C000180876

Looking at Lysistrata

LOOKING AT LYSISTRATA

Eight essays and a new
version of Aristophanes'
provocative comedy

Edited by David Stuttard

Bristol Classical Press

This impression 2011
First published in 2010 by
Bristol Classical Press
an imprint of
Bloomsbury Academic
Bloomsbury Publishing Plc
36 Soho Square,
London W1D 3QY, UK
&
175 Fifth Avenue,
New York, NY 10010, USA

Introduction and editorial arrangement
© 2010 by David Stuttard
Lysistrata, or *Loose Strife*
© 2010 by David Stuttard
The contributors retain copyright in their
individual contributions.

All rights reserved. No part of this publication
may be reproduced, stored in a retrieval system, or
transmitted, in any form or by any means, electronic,
mechanical, photocopying, recording or otherwise,
without the prior permission of the publisher.

Caution
All rights whatsoever in this play are strictly reserved.
Application for performance etc. should be made
before rehearsals to Bristol Classical Press
at the address above.

A catalogue record for this book is available
from the British Library

ISBN 978 1 85399 736 5

Typeset by Ray Davies
Printed and bound in Great Britain by
CPI Antony Rowe, Chippenham and Eastbourne

www.bloomsburyacademic.com

Contents

To EJ

Acknowledgements

My experience of staging *Lysistrata* goes back to 1996, when I translated and directed several scenes as part of my play *Blow Your Mind, Aristophanes*, performed by Actors of Dionysus at London's Mermaid Theatre in association with Tariq Ali, Channel 4 Television and the British Film Institute. To all involved then, and to all who have subsequently performed these scenes or taken part in workshops or readings of the entire script, a big thank you for helping me to see how the play actually works. Thank you, too, to those individuals with whom I have discussed the script – not least James Albrecht, Tom Davidson, Richard Dyball, Mark Katz, Sam Moorhead, Tony Ravenhall, Tamsin Shasha, Matt Smith and Ian Angus Wilkie.

The core of this volume is the essays, and unreserved thanks are due to all the contributors, both for giving so generously of their time and knowledge and for standing so firmly by the project during its long gestation period. Special thanks must go to Alan Beale, who brokered the marriage between manuscript and publisher, to Duckworth for taking it on and especially to Deborah Blake, the Editorial Director, for her excellent and unstinting work in turning it into such a handsome book. This is one time you can, perhaps, judge a book by its cover, and thanks for the striking image go to the model, Laura Williams, and photographer Dave Ashton.

Finally, my personal thanks to my partner Emily-Jane Birtwell, who, while possessing the wisdom, efficiency and organisational skills of a Lysistrata, so generously supports me in all I do.

Contributors

Alan Beale is Tutor, NE Centre for Lifelong Learning.

Edith Hall is Research Professor at Royal Holloway University of London.

Lorna Hardwick is Professor of Classical Studies and Director of the Reception of Classical Texts research project at the Open University.

James Morwood is an Emeritus Fellow of Wadham College, Oxford.

Martin Revermann is Associate Professor of Classics and Theatre Studies at the University of Toronto.

James Robson is Senior Lecturer in Classical Studies at the Open University.

Alan Sommerstein is Professor of Greek at the University of Nottingham.

David Stuttard is a freelance classicist, dramatist and writer.

J. Michael Walton is Emeritus Professor of Drama at the University of Hull.

An Introduction to *Lysistrata*

David Stuttard

The eight essays contained in this collection look at different aspects of Aristophanes' *Lysistrata*, a play which has now, at the beginning of the twenty-first century, become increasingly popular and increasingly misunderstood. Part of the reason for this popularity and misunderstanding is that readers, directors and audiences are readily seduced by the play's attractive packaging (the 'make love not war' theme), see it as surprisingly modern, and, as a result, too easily overlook the social and political context in which it was written. In this introduction, I shall briefly set *Lysistrata* in its historical context, as well as considering what Aristophanes' aims may have been when he wrote it.

Production context

Lysistrata was first performed in Athens in early 411 BC probably at the Lenaea, one of two annual Athenian religious festivals of drama sacred to the god Dionysus. Both festivals included tragedies and satyr plays (a sub-genre of comedy with plots set in the world of mythology), as well as comedies. Comedies were not just funny; they were intensely political in nature, often using the veil of humour to make serious comments about important issues of the day. As James Morwood reminds us in his contribution to this collection, Aristophanes himself commented in his *Acharnians* (performed in 425 BC), 'Comedy too [i.e. as well as tragedy] knows about justice' (line 500). Whatever the type of drama performed, in a political world com-

1

pletely dominated by men, the actors and choruses were all male. It is possible that the audiences were, too.

Because it was held in the month roughly corresponding to our January, the Lenaea was purely for the local community – at that time of year the sea was too unpredictable to allow foreign visitors to attend. *Lysistrata* was therefore aimed exclusively at an Athenian (male?) audience, whose shared experience added to its sense of intimacy and immediacy.

Of course, preparations for the production had begun much earlier. The previous summer (412 BC), Aristophanes would have submitted his proposal for inclusion in the festival, part of which may have included the reading of passages from the script. For a comic writer, this must have presented its own challenges, because much of the humour of the play relied on up-to-the-minute jokes about topical events. So we must assume that it was accepted that the script was fluid and that additions might be made right up to the day of the performance. But it does mean that the overarching theme of *Lysistrata* – that the women of Greece vote to withhold sex from their men-folk until such times as they have concluded a peace settlement – had probably been decided some six months in advance of the first performance.

Historical context

The period leading up to the first performance of *Lysistrata* is one of the most complex in Athenian history. Events were moving rapidly and the situation was changing almost daily.

Athens was at war. Since 431 BC, along with the subject states which made up the Athenian empire, Athens had been waging what we now know as the Peloponnesian War against a confederacy of other Greek states led by Sparta. Because the Athenians held supremacy at sea and the Spartan Confederacy on land, the war had been inconclusive. Indeed, in 421 BC a treaty had been signed, which led to a nominal peace lasting some eight years, but which was in fact more like a cold war, with each side becoming increasingly involved in proxy wars.

The most serious of all these involvements in proxy wars took place in Sicily, much of which had long been colonised by

Greeks. In 415 BC, a supremely confident Athens sent a large expeditionary force with the intention of defeating the island's richest city, Syracuse. But things quickly went wrong. One of the three generals, Alcibiades, was summoned back to Athens to stand trial on the capital charge of sacrilege. Instead, he escaped to Sparta, where he fed useful intelligence to the enemy. Another of the generals was killed, and the third, who had resisted the expedition from the start, mishandled it completely. A further task force was sent out, but things went from bad to worse. First the Athenian navy, then the army was annihilated. When the news reached Athens in September 413 BC it seemed to many as if defeat at the hands of the Spartans (with whom they were now again 'officially' at war) was inevitable.

But the Spartans failed to capitalise on Athens' misfortunes, and, with their backs to the wall, the Athenians worked frantic- ally to build more warships and equip more men, making massive inroads into their reserve war fund (kept in reality, as in *Lysistrata*, on the Acropolis). At the same time, the Athenian democracy voted to appoint a new board of experienced magis- trates, the *probouloi*, to help bring continuity to the war effort. One of these *probouloi* was the tragedian Sophocles. Another *proboulos*, this time a fictional one, appears in *Lysistrata* as the bungling Magistrate.

Meanwhile, some of the islands and cities in the Eastern Mediterranean and on the west coast of modern Turkey, which had long resented being subject to the Athenian em- pire, took the opportunity to try to gain their independence. Already, in July 412 BC, the Athenian navy had intercepted a Spartan fleet sailing to the island of Lesbos with the inten- tion of helping it break away from the Athenian empire, and before long Alcibiades (now working for the Spartans) had succeeded in prising another important island, Chios, away from Athens.

Such, then, was the situation when Aristophanes was plan- ning *Lysistrata* and submitting it for inclusion in the Lenaea festival: in the previous few years, a sizeable proportion of the Athenian male population had been killed in Sicily; as a result, many women had been widowed and their households severely disrupted as their legal guardianship had been transferred to surviving male relatives; defeat for Athens had been a very real possibility; it had not come, but, although there was now cause for renewed optimism, the empire was in danger of unravelling; this could make the situation much worse, especially as supplies of money with which to fund the war were running dangerously low.

In the months between *Lysistrata* being accepted for the Lenaea and its performance there in January 411 BC, the kaleidoscope of fortunes and allegiances shifted dramatically and often. As Aristophanes' actors and choruses were learning their lines and choreography, news was pouring into Athens almost by the day: the crucial city of Miletus had revolted; Athenian domination over other cities in Ionia, Caria and the nearby islands was collapsing like a house of cards; Alcibiades was negotiating a treaty between the Spartans and the Persians; he had changed sides again and was now serving the Persian governor, Tissaphernes; and, despite the odd Athenian victory, in January 411 BC (perhaps too late for news to have reached Athens by the time of the Lenaea) the powerful island of Rhodes went over to the Spartans.

So, by the time *Lysistrata* was first performed, the situation was this: many of the poorer Athenian males were now manning the warships in the Eastern Mediterranean; Athens was haemorrhaging its 'allies' and subject states at an alarming rate; and Sparta seemed to be entering into an alliance with the Persians.

Political repercussions

With many of the poorer classes gone from Athens, and faced with an empire in potential meltdown, some of the wealthier, more 'aristocratic' citizens (the class to which Aristophanes himself belonged, though there is no reason to suspect his involvement) began plotting to overthrow the Athenian democracy, impose an oligarchy and make peace with Sparta.

A number of considerations motivated them. There were undoubtedly some who were innately hostile to the very idea of the common people holding all the power; others saw how impossible it was in a war situation, when every major decision was taken by public vote, to keep secrets from the enemy; still others were concerned that, as Athenian finances were being bled dry, and as they themselves would increasingly have to foot the bill, they should have more say in the way the money would be spent; there was even an increasing number of people who thought that the only way to restore Athens' greatness was to come to terms with the exiled traitor Alcibiades, and the only way he would return would be if the democracy were overthrown. But one worry must have united them all: that the eastern superpower of Persia would become involved in the war on Sparta's side.

By June 411 BC, only five months after the first performance of *Lysistrata*, these oligarchs had created such a feeling of terror in Athens that they were, indeed, able to seize power and for a short time imposed the savage rule of 'The Four Hundred', a despotic regime which was soon superseded by the more lenient 'Five Thousand', which in turn gave way to a restored democracy. Under these oligarchic regimes, Alcibiades was indeed recalled, and peace was twice sought from the Spartans, who twice rejected the proposals.

Fantasy and reality: the 'message of *Lysistrata*'

How does this all fit in with *Lysistrata*? To find one answer, we must, I believe, turn to Plato's *Symposium,* written some time after 385 BC. In it, real characters from late fifth-century Athens discuss the nature of *eros* (loosely translated as 'love', but which more often than not means 'lust' or 'sexual attraction'). The setting is the victory party of the tragedian, Agathon, in 416 BC – five years before *Lysistrata* – and one of the characters is Aristophanes. In his fictional narrative, Plato gives Aristophanes an intriguing speech. Taking into account the fact that some of those who first read or heard the *Symposium* may have known Aristophanes, it is likely that it is true to the spirit of the sort of thing he might have been expected to say in such a context, and to the way in which he might have couched his arguments in parables.

Aristophanes' explanation of *eros* is this: in the beginning,

5

the earth was populated by spherical creatures, rolling around with two heads, four arms and four legs. There were three sexes: male, female and hermaphrodite (beings which possessed both male and female attributes). But when they became too ambitious and tried to depose Zeus from power, Zeus first considered destroying them utterly. Then, when he realised that without these creatures the gods would have no one to offer sacrifices to them, he decided on an alternative plan. He split each of the creatures into two, thus instantly halving their power and doubling the number of those who could potentially make sacrifice to the gods. Another result was that thereafter each person, aware that they were incomplete, would search for their 'other half' to make them feel whole again. *Eros* is, then, the yearning for this other half, and, depending on the gender of the original 'double' creature from which they were formed, humans might be gay, lesbian or straight.

Lysistrata, too, is on the face of it about mankind's impulse for sexual union, and about overcoming every barrier to achieve it. The women refuse their men-folk sex. The men become frustrated. Hostilities ensue. When the men can bear their abstinence no longer, they enter into negotiations. Harmony between the sexes is restored and, with it, sexual relations. But the fantasy is played out against the background of a real situation: the Peloponnesian War. In Aristophanes' equation, the restoration of sexual relations between men and women equals the restoration of peace between the warring states. Peace is preferable to fighting; make love not war. But I would argue that there is more to it than this, and that Aristophanes is, in fact, making a very serious and timely political point. He puts it into the mouth of Lysistrata herself, who, towards the end of the play has a speech, which appears in my version as:

> You all ... share one country and one history, one family, all of you, all Greeks all worshipping as one, competing all as one in the Olympic Games, with all of your achievements, Delphi and Thermopylae, art, architecture, literature, this special, wonderful, so fragile glory that is Greece – our enemies are arming themselves even as we speak, and what do you do? Slaughter Greek men, sack Greek cities. (*corresponding to lines 1128ff.*)

6

In this speech, as well as in the subsequent songs which celebrate how both Athens and Sparta managed to overcome difficulties in the past, but only with one another's help, we find ourselves straddling the real world of 411 BC and the speech which Plato ascribes to Aristophanes in his *Symposium*. Just as in the *Symposium*, the creatures, which were strong when they were whole, seek (now that they are divided) to regain that strength through physical union, so Athens, Sparta and the other Greek states were strong when they were united – strong enough to beat off the Persian invaders at the beginning of the fifth century BC. But now that they are divided (like the creatures in the *Symposium*), they are weak. And just as the gods prefer human creatures to be weak, so that they can dominate them, in the same way the Persians (the enemies to which Lysistrata refers) prefer Greece when *it* is weak, so *they* can dominate *it*.

In *Lysistrata* then, Aristophanes is making a very specific point to a very specific audience at a very specific time: if you allow *this* war to drag on, you will simply be weakening Greece and leaving us all open to an attack by the Persians. In fact, this was precisely the advice which the renegade Alcibiades, currently on the run from both Athens and Sparta had given (or was believed to have given) his new Persian master, Tissaphernes, the year before (412 BC). As Plutarch writes in his *Life of Alcibiades* (ch. 25) he

> advised them not to help [the Spartans] too readily, nor yet to destroy the Athenians, but instead through inadequate funding to cause both sides problems and slowly to wear them out, so that, when they had weakened and exhausted each other, they might become easy pickings for the Persian King.

United, Greece might stand. Divided, it would certainly fall. It was as much in the interests of the Persians to keep Athens and Sparta apart as it was in the interests of Zeus to separate the once-strong spherical creatures of the *Symposium*. In pointing this out, Aristophanes is, of course, not presenting any kind of road-map to peace. Instead, as contributors such as Alan Sommerstein show in this collection, he is simply expressing a general truth, that Greece is better off united than divided.

7

(Aristophanes' pan-Hellenic vision is discussed in this volume by James Robson and Lorna Hardwick.)

Perhaps Plato in his *Symposium* was actually reproducing the sort of arguments or parables, which he (or members of his circle) had heard the real Aristophanes voicing around the time that the *Symposium* was set. He might even be giving us a dim recollection of the meaning which Aristophanes or some of his audience placed on the scenario of *Lysistrata*. But, as we have seen, despite the seductive delights of an admittedly utopian reconciliation which Aristophanes held out to them in *Lysistrata*, the Athenians could not make peace with Sparta. The war dragged on, until, in 404 BC (seven years after *Lysistrata*), Athens was defeated by Sparta and her allies. Even this did not herald harmony in Greece, and states continued to squabble among themselves until they were so weakened that they fell easy prey to a foreign invader – not the Persians, but the Macedonians under Philip II (338 BC). They would never again enjoy the autonomy they had possessed in 411 BC. Aristophanes' prediction had, at last, come true.

Lysistrata for a modern audience

Despite being deeply rooted in its own time, *Lysistrata* has attained great popularity today, thanks in part to the belief that it is about women's emancipation, sex and an opposition to war. This has led to its being the most regularly staged of any of Aristophanes' comedies, a statistic which was greatly enhanced by its many performances worldwide in the anti-Iraq War 'Lysistrata Project' on 3 March 2003. (In this collection, the Lysistrata Project is discussed by both Lorna Hardwick and Martin Revermann.)

Partly because it is so difficult for any one translation to convey every aspect of the original, new English *Lysistrata*s are constantly appearing. Translating, adapting or writing any sort of version of the play can be a daunting task. Not only are there the obvious problems of tackling jokes which contained, for the fifth-century BC Athenian audience, up-to-the-minute topical references (often about people actually sitting in the audience), there are the more general socio-political assumptions, many of them completely alien to us, which are at the core of much of the humour – not to mention the linguistic jokes and puns – while at a deeper level, the endemic racism and sexism, which Aristophanes' plays take for granted, is alienating to most enlightened modern readers.

The more academically accurate the translation of an Aristophanic comedy, the less true to the mood and thrust of the original it is likely to be. Equally, though, the looser the version, the further it might depart from Aristophanes' intention. In my own version, I have created a parallel world, the foundation of which is fifth-century Athens, but which is inhabited by characters with an experience of early twenty-first-century British history and *mores*. It is a world which is at first sight, perhaps, more suited to that of Aristophanes' more fantastical plays like *Birds* or *Frogs*. But in reality the world of *Lysistrata*, with its dominant women, its priapic men, its free travel between Sparta or Thebes and Athens, is no less of a fantasy world than the Cloud-Cuckoo-Land of *Birds*. It is an amalgam which, if we suspend our disbelief, somehow works. I hope the same holds true for the world of my version.

Comedy ages at an alarming speed, and topical jokes quickly become stale. Should anyone (subject to observation of performance rights) wish to stage the version contained in this volume, they are encouraged to make such alterations as necessary to the few references which I have included in it to characters or events of the early twenty-first century. Furthermore, should they wish to remove references and jokes which appear to them to be too Anglocentric and replace them with others more appropriate to their own setting, they are welcome to do this, too, if during the process they consult me. (This can be done through the publisher.)

The essays

This volume contains eight essays written by some of the leading authorities on *Lysistrata* today, addressing a diverse range of issues, from the structure of the play to the way in which it reflects fifth-century BC society, to its reception in modern productions by contemporary audiences. The authors were allowed total freedom to choose what aspect of the play to write on, and, for the most part, each was unaware of what the others intended to say. For this reason, there is occasionally some overlap between one or two of the essays. To preserve the integrity of each piece, I have deliberately not removed such overlaps. Indeed, I believe that they are in themselves illuminating. For, read individually, each essay is stimulating and informative; taken together, they provide a compelling overview of scholarly thinking about the play at the end of the first decade of the twenty-first century.

1

Where is the Spine?

J. Michael Walton

Many theatre directors, when facing the challenge of reviving a classic or classical text, will look for what they call the play's 'spine', by which they mean the central issue which will inform and lead their production. This is not to suggest that a play can have only one spine. Far from it. The greater the play, it often seems, the more opportunities to select and highlight an approach which individualises and autographs one production rather than any other, sometimes discovering new elements, sometimes offering a new perspective on familiar ones.

Such factors may be quite simple; they may be complex. In writing about Aristophanes' *Lysistrata* I want to give some indication of what lies behind this comedy, first performed in Athens in 411 BC and probably not again anywhere until its return to the same city in 1904. What is it that enables such a play still to speak to us in the twenty-first century, when for so many hundreds of years it was some sort of pariah piece that classicists preferred to disown? Where are the spines of *Lysistrata* for us today? In sexual politics? In cultural identity? In anti-war protest? Or simply in its theatrical gusto and bawdy humour?

One of the requirements for a Greek tragedy identified by Aristotle in his *Poetics* was that it should be *spoudaios*, 'worth taking seriously'. Whatever Aristotle wrote about comedy has not survived, but any reading of Aristophanes, and no play more than *Lysistrata*, shows that in ancient Athens comedy too was a serious business.

11

J. Michael Walton

Aristophanes and his time

Had he no place in the history of theatre, Aristophanes would still repay close study as a social historian. No other writer from the fifth century BC offers more insights into the concerns and preoccupations of his fellow Athenians.

Consider only some of the plots of the eleven of his plays which have survived. A farmer is so fed up with trying to make a living in wartime that he organises a private peace treaty with Sparta and declares his farm a war-free zone (*Acharnians*, 425 BC); a father enrols his son in Socrates' 'College' so that he can learn how to avoid paying his debts (*Clouds*, 423 BC or later); a son attempts to restrain his father who has become addicted to the lawcourts (*Wasps*, 422 BC); another farmer fattens up a dung-beetle and flies up to heaven to save the goddess Peace who has been thrown down a well by War (*Peace*, 421 BC); two Athenians leave Athens and found a new city in mid-air, a city of birds (*Birds*, 414 BC): and all these before he ever wrote *Lysistrata*.

What an imagination! What a challenge to the staging resources of his own time and the theatrical sophistication of an audience who had come to learn in less than a hundred years the basic ground-rules of this new art-form of drama which combined mask, music and dance: and, within this form known as Old Comedy, of which Aristophanes was the best-known proponent, add parody, irreverence, gags of all kinds, hard politics and pure fantasy.

Despite the range of his situations, it is not difficult to pick up the one recurrent theme which links *Lysistrata* (411 BC) to much of the earlier work: namely, the war against Sparta. If Aristophanes tells us what exercised the ordinary Athenian in his or her (filtered through a decidedly male gaze) day-by-day concerns, he also gives a better impression than anyone else of what it must have been like to be alive in Attica during the Peloponnesian War (431-404 BC). Biographical details of any of the Greek playwrights are vague, but Aristophanes was at most nineteen years of age, and may have been only fourteen, when the war broke out. It is likely that he fought in it at some time. Yet, in play after play, he shows opposition to this conflict from ordinary men and women from the city and the countryside of

12

Attica whose lives were blighted by the conceits of metropolitan war-mongers and politicians. In this he matches his near-contemporary, the playwright Euripides, many of whose tragedies show a similar aversion to the processes and effects of war.

Seven years after *Lysistrata*, and following closely on the deaths of both Sophocles and Euripides in 405 BC, Aristophanes was to create perhaps his most extravagant flight of fancy when, in *Frogs* (404 BC), Dionysus, the god of theatre himself, visits Hades to bring back a playwright to save the city of Athens. After a fiercely-fought competition between Aeschylus and Euripides based on their merits as playwrights, Dionysus chooses to bring back Aeschylus, the older tragedian. Aeschylus and Dionysus set off back to the upper world, with the devout hope expressed by Pluto, god of the underworld, ringing in their ears, that all those incompetent politicians who want to continue the war will be packed off down to Hades as soon as possible.

But it was *Lysistrata*, not *Frogs* nor any other Aristophanic comedy, which over the years was to acquire a special notoriety.

Lysistrata and its reputation

The play's central situation has proved to be both the strength and the weakness behind its subsequent notoriety. The plot can be summed up quite briefly. An Athenian matron, Lysistrata, is so angry with the way in which men have devastated Greece through their enthusiasm for the war against Sparta that she marshals a group of women and gets them to agree to an embargo on sex with their husbands until peace is declared. In the simplicity of this set-up resides its strength.

The women, incidentally, are not simply Athenians, but include representatives from Sparta, Boeotia and Corinth against whom Athens and her allies have been ranged on the battlefield on and off for the last twenty years. The decision for a sex-strike proves predictably difficult to implement and most of the play is taken up with the comic implications, both physical and emotional, of trying to 'down tools'. There are numerous jokes about erections which, though not especially shocking now, are still funny if somewhat relentless.

It has not always seemed so, as a brief account of the play's translation history and stage revival can demonstrate. The apparent obsession with sex identifies the play's weakness and accounts for the hostile reception it received over so many hundred years. Times have changed, as has the direction of obsession with sex, which now dominates television ratings and newspaper sales with a prurient mixture of moralistic fervour and unmitigated hypocrisy that the ancient Greeks would have been utterly incapable of comprehending.

Translation

Aristophanes himself survived the fall of Athens in 404 BC and went on to write more plays, two of which have survived. But the tone has changed and, more obviously, so has the political dimension. Most of the references to contemporary politicians, so blatant in the earlier work, have gone by the wayside, perhaps through the pressures of a more edgy era. It used to be thought that Aristophanes' plays were too parochial to have travelled far outside Athens. More recent scholarship suggests that he was just as popular among the Greek colonies of southern Italy. Concerns over mainly Athenian affairs, however, led to a demise of his type of fantastic farce in favour of the more amiable social comedy of Menander and his fellows. Nor was Aristophanes much use as a teaching text in later times. His plays did survive in libraries but were for years effectively disparaged by literary critics, or ignored.

Tragedy was different. Though Seneca, in the more accessible Latin, proved the inspiration for much Renaissance tragedy, Greek myth did provide a source of much original work. Greek comedy and Roman comedy, based on the Greek, for the most part avoided mythological plots. By the time of the Restoration occasional translations of the plays of Aeschylus, Sophocles and Euripides were beginning to see the light of day, though the big breakthrough in this field was not until 1759 when Charlotte Lennox translated from French into English Father Pierre Brumoy's massive three-volume work on Greek Theatre. This contained either a resumé or a complete translation of every surviving Greek tragedy. When it came to comedy, Lennox was so uncomfortable that she abdicated responsibility to other, and male, hands. A bare seven and a half pages are devoted to Aristophanes' *Lysistrata*, with quotations from the text amounting to only thirteen lines, all grudgingly introduced with the following disclaimer:

> This comedy, as well in its plan as most of its circumstances, lies open to the censures of criticism; we neither can nor ought to dwell upon it .... He would doubtless have been more deserving of our esteem, if he had not disgraced the noble freedom of his comic muse by a shocking licentiousness, and by abominable pictures which will always render him the horror and execration of every reader who has the least taste for modesty and delicacy of sentiment.

Not surprisingly, the first published translations of Aristophanes pointedly ignored *Lysistrata*, which did not appear in English until 1837. Then, Charles Wheelwright offered some 'Preliminary Observations' which began thus: 'The *Lysistrata* bears so evil a character that we must make but fugitive mention of it, like persons passing over hot embers.' Wheelwright's translation is anyway peppered with asterisks and expurgations, greeted by such comments as 'Here twenty-five lines are omitted', culminating in 'omitted from lines 828 to line 1215'. That's nearly a quarter of the whole play!

The first translation of *Lysistrata* which claimed to be of the whole text (by Samuel Smith) was not printed until 1896, and then as a limited edition of sophisticated pornography, with exceptionally graphic, anatomically improbable and barely relevant illustrations from Aubrey Beardsley. The actual text is surprisingly bland.

Stage revival

If Aristophanes' situations and dialogue were regarded as far too salty for publication, the British theatre, beset as it was until 1968 by the stringent control of the office of the Lord Chamberlain as censor, was certainly not going to allow anyone to witness the play on a public stage. Even between the two World Wars, no production was allowed: none, in fact, until

1957 when the Dudley Fitts translation was produced for the English Stage Company by Greek director Minos Volonakis. That was condemned as 'savagely pornographic' by the monthly periodical *Theatre World*. By 1993 a production of the play by Peter Hall, in a translation from Ranjit Bolt, raised few eyebrows for the sexual content, but was criticised in *Plays and Players* as being 'soaked in clever cultural parallels, risking the loss of the evening's dangerous edge in a cluster of safe and tasteful references', an interesting reflection on 'modernising'.

Nevertheless, when a call went out from two New York academics in 2003 for an international protest against the war in Iraq through theatre performance, *Lysistrata* was the play they chose. On the same day, 3 March of that year (3/3/3), over a thousand separate readings or productions were played world-wide, from India to Chile, Iceland to Japan.

If Aristophanes has lost the power to shock through his sexual and scatalogical references, he can now at last, as never before, offer comic parables on aspects of contemporary living.

Sex or politics?

What makes *Lysistrata* a special case in the present context is not so much that it is about sex, as that people think it is only about sex. The history of stage comedy has tended to find much greater mileage in people failing to have sex than in having it. As Aristophanes amply demonstrates in the scene between Myrrhine and Kinesias, prevention is funnier than consummation. The women of Athens decide not to sleep with their husbands until peace is declared: as simple as that. The fact that Athenian men at the time notoriously had recourse to several alternative outlets for their energies and urges is simply a dramatic irrelevance.

But within the play, sex, or lack of it, is only a means to an end. Women, or at least the stage women of Aristophanes, need to employ the most potent weapon that they have in order to get what they want. And the most potent weapon they have is the thwarting of male potency. It is often suggested that Aristophanes is making fun of women. After all he did write a whole comedy called *Festival Time* (*Thesmophoriazusae*) about the goings-on at the women-only festival of the Thesmophoria, a play which was actually produced in the same year as *Lysistrata*, though at a different festival. It seems just as likely that what he reveals here is not so much a contempt for women as a fear of them and what they might get up to, latent within the male citizens of ancient Athens.

The women want an end to the war. That is a serious issue, the most serious issue of any in the Athens of 411 BC, reeling from the appalling losses of the failed Sicilian expedition. How they achieve this may make an audience laugh, but it doesn't make the purpose any less important.

The consequent deprivation experienced by the female characters, never mind the male, has to be measured against one major factor. The play was originally written to be performed by an all-male cast. *Lysistrata* is a 'drag' play. Apart from one scene and a few references to the visible signs of arousal it is not really much more sexy than many a Carry On film or television sitcom. Its mood is more that of Christmas pantomime, with male cross-dressing (though not female), slapstick and plenty of innuendo.

One of Aristophanes' late plays, *Women in Assembly* (*Ecclesiazusae*, 392 BC), amplifies the playwright's enthusiasm for exploiting the comic dimension of cross-dressing. The central situation is not so dissimilar to that of *Lysistrata*. The women of Athens are again frustrated by the male domination in government. One of their number, Praxagora, persuades them to get up early and go in disguise to the Assembly and vote women into control of the city, which they do, and the play deals with the consequences. It is the theatrical situation that is intriguing here, a splendid development on the men dressed as women who feature in *Lysistrata* and elsewhere. The first characters to appear are the women of Athens, male actors dressed up as women who have disguised themselves as men in their husbands' clothes. As soon as they have left for the Assembly, the husbands arrive, dressed as women. They have been unable to find their own clothes and have had to put on their wives' instead. How confusing can you get?

Is there any more profound message in *Lysistrata*? Perhaps, but it is difficult to find any real feminist statement within an Aristophanes play. They were written for male masked actors and it may be possible to make some distinction between the 'drag' characters and the 'sexy' ones. Lysistrata herself, whose name translated means 'Freer of the Army' is much more 'Dame' than 'Principal Girl'. The character Reconciliation, on the other hand, who has no lines and whose presence, apparently naked, is required largely to invite lewd comments from the men, could even have been played by a real woman. Though there were no actresses as such in the Greek theatre, there are frequent occasions when a non-speaking character's appearance implies specific female attributes. Young female slaves, dancers and barmaids were a regular feature of otherwise all-male social gatherings, so why not the theatre of festival too?

But this is pure speculation. Many of the original conditions of performance are simply unknown. Logic would suggest that a restriction on the number of masked actors to three, if indeed, it was an absolute for tragedy, could not have been so for comedy. The surviving plays of the New Comedy writer Menander appear to have been created for a company of five and several of Aristophanes, including *Lysistrata,* seem to require at least the same number.

Lysistrata today

Beyond any considerations about the first production is the really important issue for the modern translator or director of trying to recreate the unusual balance between the riotous and the thought-provoking. Aristophanes is ill-served by being reduced to a romp. At the same time he is writing comedy. It may be arguable whether the playwright's sense of farce with a purpose needs reproducing today when so much of audience expectation has altered. On the other hand, if all we are looking for is a few camp jokes, why bother with such an old play in the first place? Somewhere along the line, in every Aristophanes play that has survived, are moments of truth to make us wince. Hardly a member of that first audience, it must be remembered, would not have not lost a father, brother or son in a war that seemed to be heading nowhere, The laughter in *Lysistrata* is underscored by tears.

1. Where is the Spine?

One way of 'modernising' may be to look for parallels from the present and to update the play to a current situation by a wholesale transfer to today's politicians and today's voices of protest. But to be so explicit, I believe, diminishes the power of the original which manages to hit home even though it is rooted in ancient Athens. Jokes about 'the war on terror' or Iraq may seem to have immediacy, but date as quickly as have jokes about the World Wars, Korea or Vietnam. *Lysistrata*, at this distance, is less about one war than about War, as War is personified as a character in Aristophanes' *Peace*. In other words, the message is universal not specific. Not that this implies any enthusiasm for an archaeological revival. What could be more deadly? Let the jokes be of any time as long as they are funny. Let the message too be for any time so that the play becomes, not a piece of instant propaganda, but a true comment on the human enthusiasm for destruction and how it may be challenged.

In all of this, if we want to find our 'spine', there is some balance to be reached between the sex jokes, the socio-political satire and serious comment on war and the conduct of war. There are issues behind this play, serious issues, though located in a stage world whose conventions were established more than two thousand four hundred years ago. The remarkable thing is that Aristophanes can still stretch out over so many centuries and cultures and offer some laughs and, among the laughs, something of the unease of all true comedy.

The Upside-down World of Aristophanes' *Lysistrata*

James Morwood

In a famous line from his *Acharnians* (425 BC) Aristophanes' hero Dikaiopolis (whose name means 'honest citizen') makes the claim that

> Comedy too [i.e. as well as tragedy] knows about justice. (500)

The comic protagonist insists here on the *seriousness* of comedy, the fact that it too has important things to say about the human condition. And indeed I find myself wondering at times whether it can communicate that condition *more* fully and truthfully than tragedy. It may be that the great nineteenth-century actor Edmund Kean hit the nail on the head when he declared:

> No, no, you may humbug the town some time longer as a trage-
> dian, but comedy is a serious thing.

Comedy is after all an essential part of the business of living. When Sir Philip Sidney wrote in his *Defence of Poesie* (publish-ed posthumously in 1595) of the works of modern playwrights 'mingling Kinges and Clownes', he was making a trenchant criticism of what he saw as their violation of dramatic decorum; but in fact he was surely putting his finger on a key ingredient of the greatness of Shakespeare, for one.

So is Aristophanes' uproarious comedy *Lysistrata* 'a serious thing', to employ Kean's terminology? Certainly the anti-war message that it puts across is deadly serious. It was staged in

2. The Upside-down World of Aristophanes' Lysistrata

411 BC, at what was for Athens a grim time in the Peloponnesian War, her long drawn-out conflict with the Spartan-led confederacy. Two of Athens' armies and fleets had been annihilated in 413 in the final throes of her disastrous expedition to Sicily. In order to build a new fleet, the Athenians had spent their emergency reserve of 1,000 talents. Their allies were abandoning them in droves. Within sight of Athens there was a Spartan garrison which confined them to the fortified area of the city and its harbour, and cut them off from their agricultural land and their silver mines.[1] Later in 411, their loss of control of the neighbouring island of Euboea was, according to the historian Thucydides, to cause unprecedented panic in the city (8.96.1). But her enemies' lack of initiative postponed disaster, the historian remarking laconically that 'on this occasion, as on many others, the Spartans proved to be the most helpful enemies that the Athenians could have had' (8.96.5). The city held out for another seven years.

However, the seriousness of the play's comedy applies to far more than the alarming historical background against which Lysistrata is seen organising her international female sex-strike in order to force the men to make peace. Through his pervasive deployment of the concept of festival, Aristophanes gives full rein to the expression of patterns of human behaviour that have deep anthropological roots. Thus his comedy is serious in the sense that it embodies fundamental truths about the life experience. In a lively and illuminating book, Paul Cartledge shows how he summons up the spirit of festival.[2] And in his rewarding study of the playwright, Angus Bowie examines the ways in which Aristophanes' work is informed by various Athenian and Greek festivals.[3] Especially relevant to Lysistrata are the all-female Thesmophoria,[4] the festival of Adonis and the New Fire Festival on Lemnos. Bowie's book will fill you in on these fascinating festivals.

The play's evocation of the festive spirit finds expression of a very obvious kind in such features as the earthy bawdiness of its language and the erect phalli that the male characters sport from l.845 on (the phalli of comedy normally droop). It is also a feature of the topsy-turvy world that the play presents. Indeed, the concept of reversal is the comedy's life blood. This comes

21

across in the detail. When the women from all over Greece swear to refuse their husbands sex, they take their oath not over the customary shield but over a wine cup, and they pour wine into it, not blood (195-239). The substitutions ram home the comedy's plea for peace. But the play as a whole is informed by a fundamental reversal of roles between women and men. The women appropriate masculine functions. They become soldiers (241ff.), seizing the Acropolis, arming themselves (454) and taking control of the treasury so that the war can no longer be funded (488-97). They make the chorus of old men back off, defeat them, and then take the initiative in effecting a reconciliation. They drive off the police force (435-49). As we have seen, they make an international treaty. Crucially, Lysistrata makes the claim that war *is* women's concern. When the Magistrate asserts that they have had no part at all in the war, she trenchantly points out that they bear sons and send them out as warriors (588-90).

There are surely two intertextual references here. One of them is to Medea's famous declaration in Euripides' play that she would prefer to stand in the battle line three times than to give birth once (*Medea* 250-1). In drawing this contrast, Medea makes a firm distinction between male and female roles. Lysistrata on the other hand is pointing out that the fact that women give birth to the warriors actually involves them in the warfare. The other intertextual reference is to the celebrated episode in Homer's *Iliad* when Hector sends his wife Andromache back home to the loom. 'War will be the concern of all the men,' he declares (*Iliad* 6.490-3: cf. *Lysistrata* 520). Lysistrata definitively rejects such gender stereotyping. At line 637 of Aristophanes' play, the old women strip down for battle quite literally. And the old men assert that if the women get anywhere at all with their attack,

> they will construct warships and try to fight a sea battle and ram us like Artemisia [the fighting queen of Halicarnassus]. And if they turn to horsemanship, I write off our cavalry. (674-6)

Of Artemisia the Persian king had famously said, under the mistaken impression that she had sunk an enemy ship during his defeat at the battle of Salamis, 'My men have become women, and my women men.'[5] And two lines later the old men of *Lysistrata* invite consideration of the Amazons, those famous female warriors of legend.

Perhaps even more arresting than the women's usurpation of the military sphere is their appropriation of control of sexual relations within marriage. Both of these breathtaking invasions of male areas of control are reflected in small but telling ways in the play's language. One of the women violates the conventions of Aristophanic comedy by uttering a crude word ('shit') in the presence of men (440).[6] Myrrhine usurps the male oath 'by Apollo' (917). And men refer to Lysistrata by name three times (1086, 1103, 1147) in contravention of normal Athenian etiquette which forbade a man to refer to a respectable woman in public in this way.

The corollary of all this is that the play's men are emasculated, a fact paradoxically emphasised by the painfulness of the useless erect phalli in the second half of the play. The most hilarious episode of the comedy is surely the one in which the prick-teasing Myrrhine repeatedly denies sexual satisfaction to her husband Kinesias, finally scurrying off to leave him in a state of humiliated frustration. Then Kleisthenes is a figure poised between the masculine and feminine. And before being dressed as a corpse, the Magistrate is costumed as a women (602-4, 533-7). The play's men are reduced to a state of abject surrender.

This reversal of male roles is particularly gobsmacking when one considers what the actual lives of Greek women were like. James Davidson sums up the matter like this:

Ancient Greek women lived lives that would be far more recognisable to the women of Iran or Saudi Arabia today than to the women of the modern West. Their skin was pale from a life in the shadows. When they were not indoors they covered up with a veil … Men kept well away from women they were not related to, and even husbands and wives often slept in different, sex-separated, parts of the house. Decent women were not supposed even to be spoken of in the public world of men, according to the funeral speech penned for [the politician] Pericles by [the historian] Thucydides. For a woman even to allow herself to be seen at a window or leaning over the sill of a Dutch door was dangerous for her reputation …[7]

23

As Davidson goes on to point out, this relegation of women to the cloister of the home was reflected in their exclusion from public life. They could not own land, houses or businesses. For legal and other transactions they had to work through their official male representative. And, of course, they had no role at all in politics.

So, if the reversal of male and female roles in the play is so far divorced from reality, how can I justify my claim that it is *serious*? A possible answer is that this kind of upside-down world *did* attain a reality in the ancient Greece – at festivals. For example, at the festival of Haloa at Eleusis women engaged in feasting and drinking, exchanged sexual vulgarities, handled sexual objects, and even listened to the priestesses whispering in their ear as they urged them to commit adultery.[8] For a brief period of holiday the oppressive norms of their life were suspended. However, we can find a still closer parallel to the topsy-turvy world of *Lysistrata* in the long-standing Athenian harvest festival called the Kronia[9] (Kronos was the father of Zeus). A writer called Philochorus (fourth and third centuries BC) tells us of the custom at this festival that 'in all households, when the crops and fruits were brought in, the masters should feast on them with their slaves, with whom they had shared the hard labour of cultivating the land'.[10] Accius, a Roman poet of the late second century BC, gives the further detail that masters actually waited on their slaves.[11] It has been argued that Accius is back-projecting on the Kronia the custom of masters waiting upon their slaves that was certainly a feature of the Roman winter festival of the Saturnalia. However, the fact of the matter is that a number of 'Saturnalian' festivals in Greece gave just such opportunities for the kind of reversal that liberates the oppressed. H.S. Versnel itemises a number of these:

> During the Thessalian festival of the Peloria, dedicated to Zeus Peloros, strangers were offered a banquet, prisoners freed of their fetters; slaves reclined at dinner and were waited upon by their masters, with full freedom of speech. At festivals of the god Hermes on Crete too, the slaves stuffed themselves and the masters served. Ephoros (*Fragments of Greek Historians* 70 F 29) even knows of a festival in Kydonia on Crete where

24

the serfs, the Klarotes, could lord it in the city while the citizens stayed outside. The slaves were also allowed to whip the citizens, probably those who had recklessly remained in the city or re-entered it.[12]

What is the significance of such holiday reversals for our play? Parker remarks of the Kronia:

> In the 'life in the time of Kronos' (a proverbial expression) there was no slavery; at the *Kronia* the difference between slave and master is effaced or even reversed. But the suspension of status differences cannot outlast the festival, because we live now under Zeus. Oppressive social relations that entail a certain proximity or even intimacy between oppressor and oppressed appear to create a need for reversal rituals of this type ...[13]

In a similar pattern of reversal *Lysistrata* liberates the women from male oppression. Indeed, they become the oppressors. This reflects the pattern of the festivals which allowed women playful alternatives to their normal lifestyle through ritual reversal. As Versnel puts it, 'For a short time, oppressed social groups are given an opportunity to relax pent up aggression in a game of reversed roles.'[14] But both the festivals and the comedies last a short time. The holiday is soon over. Despite the fact that she does what the men have failed to do and brings peace to the whole Greek world – or perhaps precisely because of that fact – Lysistrata is the Lady of Misrule who must bow once more to male supremacy. The reversal is reversed. The *status quo* is confirmed, even strengthened. Lysistrata herself endorses this near the play's conclusion when, even as she asserts her own wisdom, she acknowledges her debt to her education by men:

> I am a woman but I do have a mind. I am not badly off for intelligence on my own account, and I am not badly educated, having heard many words from my father and from other older men. (1124-7)

The carnival play – in both senses of the word 'play' – of women's liberation is drawing to a conclusion.

But the comedy's template of reversal remains operative

until the very end of *Lysistrata* as we now have it. While the Spartan's concluding lyric (1296-1321) is very likely to have been followed by a choral exit song, now lost, his final plea for a song to Athena, the Lady of the Bronze House (1321), invites celebration of the great goddess of Athens under her Spartan cult-name. In a recent book, Martin Revermann argues that the lyric was added for a revival of the play for a Spartan audience, possibly at Taras in Southern Italy, and asks, 'Can a comedy performed in Athens in 411 *end* with a celebratory hymn to Athena addressed in her cult function as the protectress of the arch-enemy's city which Athens is at war with at the moment?'[15] I share the majority view and feel *contra* Revermann that the answer is yes. The mind-boggling extent of Lysistrata's victory and the *entente cordiale* that she has created[16] are triumphantly celebrated in the Spartan's song in praise of the goddess of Athens in a theatrical space which was at the very heart of Athenian civic life.

Despite this endorsement of Lysistrata's triumph, however, the goddess Athena resists any type-casting as an embodiment of female domination. While the fact that she is the goddess both of warfare and of spinning and weaving reflects the role of women in the play,[17] Pheidias' two great statues of her on the Acropolis – one of them facing visitors as they entered, the other in the Parthenon itself – showed on her shield the Amazons, those archetypal female warriors, in the process of being defeated by Theseus, the king of Athens. And in a notorious speech from a dramatic trilogy that had by now become a classic, Aeschylus' *Oresteia*, Athena declares that no mother gave her birth – she sprang fully armed from the head of Zeus – and is on the side of men (*Eumenides* 736-7). We discover again that we have re-entered the world of male supremacy.

Tragically for Athens, the dream of peace was to prove as evanescent as that of women's liberation. In 410 BC, the year after *Lysistrata* was performed, the Spartans were defeated at the battle of Cyzicus and sued for peace.[18] The Athenians' victory heartened them and they took a democratic decision to reject the Spartan overtures.[19] The bitter reality was that six years later an occupying Spartan army marched up Athena's acropolis. The time for laughter was over. In Karolos Koun's memorable production of *Lysistrata* with the Greek Arts Theatre at the World Theatre Season in London in 1969, the play ended with an air raid siren sounding. Everybody on stage scurried for shelter. It was a brilliantly insightful and unfunny, indeed challengingly serious conclusion.

Notes

1. Alan H. Sommerstein (ed.), *Lysistrata* (Warminster: Aris and Phillips, 1990, revised 1998, 2007), 1.

2. *Aristophanes and his Theatre of the Absurd* (Bristol: Bristol Classical Press, 1990). Readings of the plays that invoke the spirit of festival, holiday and carnival look back to two seminal works, C.L. Barber's *Shakespeare's Festive Comedy* (Princeton: Princeton University Press, 1959) and Mikhail Bakhtin's *Rabelais and his World* (Cambridge MA: MIT Press, 1968). It was Bakhtin's study of Rabelais which popularised the idea of 'carnival consciousness', a mode of thought characterised by the temporary inversion of the categories of everyday life.

3. *Aristophanes, Myth, Ritual and Comedy* (Cambridge: Cambridge University Press, 1993).

4. Aristophanes' play set at this festival, *Thesmophoriazusae*, almost certainly dates from the same year as *Lysistrata*.

5. Herodotus 8.88.3.

6. See Sommerstein's note on this line.

7. James Davidson, *The Times Literary Supplement*, 5 October 2007, p. 3.

8. Robert Parker, *Polytheism and Society at Athens* (Oxford: Oxford University Press, 2005), 167.

9. Parker (2005) 202. Long-standing because the festival conveys the idea 'old-fashioned' at Aristophanes, *Clouds* 398.

10. Macrobius, *Saturnalia* 1.10.22 = Philochorus *Fragments of Greek Historians* 328 F 97.

11. *Ann.* F 3 M, Bae; *Fragmenta Poetarum Latinorum* Morel p. 34.

12. *Tradition and Reversal in Myth and Ritual* (Leiden: E.J. Brill, 1993), 103-4.

13. *Polytheism and Society at Athens*, 202.

14. *Tradition and Reversal in Myth and Ritual*, 115-16.

15. *Comic Business, Theatricality, Dramatic Technique, and Performance Contexts of Aristophanic Comedy* (Oxford: Oxford University Press, 2006), 258.

16. N. Loraux, *The Children of Athena: Athenian Ideas about Citi-*

zenship and the Division Between the Sexes (Princeton: Princeton University Press, 1993), 173.

17. See lines 567-86.

18. Diodorus Siculus 13.52.3, Philochorus *Fragments of Greek Historians* 328 F 139.

19. Thucydides 105.5, Diodorus Siculus 13.53.1-3.

3

The Many Faces of Lysistrata

Edith Hall

When some expert cross-dressing male actor first donned the mask and costume of Lysistrata in 411 BC, he was making theatre history. This was by far the most important female role that Aristophanes had so far composed, whether measured in terms of the number of lines, the variety of vocal and physical performance styles required by the role, or the moral and political authority which Lysistrata seems able to exert over women, men, Athenians and Spartans alike. But Lysistrata is also a sophisticated and complex figure, who shares features with several other women both in Greek myth and cult and in social reality.

The standard mythical picture of ancient Greek women in wartime depicts them as passive victims of male violence, cowering behind the walls of Troy or Thebes to await the siege of their city and enslavement. But there were plenty of assertive women in Greek myth who provide precedents for some of Lysistrata's spunky leadership qualities. The motif of the sex-strike that Lysistrata proposes and implements is already present in a story told in a short epic called *The Shield of Heracles*: Alcmena refused to have sexual intercourse with her husband until he had avenged the death of her brothers by burning down two enemy villages (4-19). Alcmena refused sex in order to create war, where Lysistrata suggests that only sexual deprivation can bring about peace. But as sex-strike initiator she has a forebear in the epic tradition.

The Aristophanic comedy can also be illuminated by the parallel provided by its plot with the various matriarchies –

societies run by women rather than men – to be found in Greek myth. The story of the Lemnian women is implicitly referred to in the play in jokes about bad smells and fire (66-8, 296-301). The women of the island of Lemnos, led by their queen Hypsipyle, had been afflicted with a bad body odour problem; as a result their husbands had become unfaithful; so the women had risen up, killed the men, and taken over the island. Aristophanes' audience knew about this story from both epic and tragedy, and was therefore familiar with the basic plotline featuring a takeover of the state by women. An even more obvious parallel is drawn in the comedy with the Amazons, the mythical warrior-women who had long ago invaded Athens and were depicted on the shield held by the great statue of Athena herself on the acropolis (Pausanias 1.17.2). They were also to be seen in a famous painting by the artist Micon that hung in another building in the city centre, and the old men in *Lysistrata* refer to this painting when they are trying to understand what their own womenfolk are doing (671-9) in attempting to take over the city.

If Lysistrata's initiative reminds the men within the play of the Lemnian women and the Amazons, Lysistrata herself feels that a stronger parallel should be drawn with the legendary wise woman, Melanippe, who knew many secrets about the gods that she divulged for the benefit of mankind.

Lysistrata uses language, especially in the scene with the magistrate, that will certainly have reminded her audience of a popular tragedy written a few years previously by the tragedian Euripides about Melanippe. This female sage had delivered a famous speech in defence of women, and against the misogynist opinions that men held about them, and a part of the speech survives:

> Men's criticism of women is worthless twanging of a bowstring and evil talk. Women are better than men, as I will show ... Consider their role in religion, for that, in my opinion, comes first. We women play the most important part, because women prophesy the will of Zeus in the oracles of Phoebus (Apollo). And at the holy site of Dodona near the sacred oak, females convey the will of Zeus to inquirers from Greece. As for the sacred rituals for the Fates and the Nameless Ones, all these would not

be holy if performed by men, but prosper in women's hands. In this way women have a rightful share in the service of the gods. Why is it, then, that women must have a bad reputation?

Lysistrata, like this famous character in a tragedy, argues that women are not evil, and we will see below that it is interesting that the major argument we know Euripides' Melanippe had used was that women are excellent at running cults and performing rituals.

Alcmena, Hypsipyle, an Amazon, or Melanippe the Wise – Lysistrata shares different features with all of these mythical women. She proposed a sex-strike, is prepared to take over the city and administer it, and is a persuasive orator on behalf of women who stresses the serious responsibilities that they are capable of carrying out. But what about history? Were there female equivalents of these assertive wives, matriarchs, warriors, and wise women in reality? In Greek historical narratives generally, women are far less directly involved in war. The historical example of female passivity most often offered is the fate of the women of Melos after the Athenians besieged their citadel in 415 BC: their adult menfolk were all killed, and they were all sold into slavery along with their children (Thucydides 5.116). But there are a few signs that women, far from sitting around waiting for events to develop, were indeed capable of intervention. Desperate times such as war breed desperate measures.

When the old men in *Lysistrata* liken the rebellious women to Amazons, they are also reminded of the real historical queen Artemisia, who had come from Asia with the Persian invasion of 480 BC, commanded a ship, and had made a great impression as a warlike female on the Greek mind. In a gripping example from closer to Lysistrata's time, the historian Thucydides relates during the civil war in Corcyra (Corfu) in 427 BC, there was a battle in the streets when the women and slaves on the side of the democratic party joined in the actual fighting: 'the woman also entered the fray with great daring, hurling down tiles from the roof-tops and standing up to the din with a courage that went beyond what was natural to their sex' (3.74).

On another occasion in the early fourth century, according to

31

a writer on war tactics called Aeneas, the citizens of the Black Sea city of Sinope were under siege; since they were so short of men, 'they disguised the most able-bodied of the women and armed them as much like men as they could, giving them in place of shields and helmets their jars and similar bronze kitchen utensils, and marched them around the wall where the enemy were most likely to see them' (*On Siegecraft* ch. 40.4-5). Here women do not actually fight, but are regarded as a resource than can be used directly in warfare, dressed up as men and opposed to the same dangers.

It was not only in Corfu and the Black Sea that women were capable of brave participation in war. When Cleomenes the Spartan climbed the Athenian acropolis in order to seize it in 506 BC, he had not expected that a lone woman would stand up to him. Herodotus reports that when he tried to enter the temple of Athena, the priestess rose from her chair to prevent him from entering, and declared 'Spartan stranger, go back! Do not enter the holy place. No Dorian is permitted to go in!' In the event Cleomenes did have to depart altogether just two days later.

The priesthood of Athena Polias – Athena in her role as protector of the city – was a very important public office, held for life, and the incumbent was traditionally supplied by one of the oldest and most respected families in Athens, the Eteoboutadai. The individual who held the office – who could not be a married woman – was always and inevitably one of the most visible and influential women in Athens, but this particular priestess, at the time of the democratic revolution, seems to have been outstandingly brave and memorable. We have some information about another woman who held the office later. In one of the most fascinating discoveries of the mid-twentieth century, an inscription was discovered that allowed us to discover the identity of the woman who was priestess at the time that *Lysistrata* was first produced. The astonishing possibility emerged that Lysistrata was directly modelled on a real woman, the priestess of Athena in 411, whose name was Lysimache. She had a brother, who also held public office, whose name was Lysicles. According to a much later source, the Roman Pliny, this Lysimache held office for 64 years (*Natural*

History 34.76)! Lysistrata means 'the woman who disbands the army', and Lysimache means something very similar, 'the woman who puts a stop to the fighting'. (See also in this volume Martin Revermann, p. 74, James Robson, p. 52 and Alan Sommerstein, p. 46.)

It seems almost impossible that the original audience of *Lysistrata* would not have made the connection between their most important priestess's name and that of Aristophanes' revolutionary new heroine. Indeed, Lysistrata herself seems to refer to the priestess when she is addressing the Magistrate: she says that since women desire men and men desire women, then she and her female comrades will be successful in their aims and 'be known amongst the Greeks as *Lysimaches*, 'the women who put a stop to the fighting' (551-4). Ten years earlier, in Aristophanes' comedy *Peace* of 421 BC, the peace-loving hero Trygaeus had prayed to the on-stage statue of the goddess Eirene (Peace) 'to resolve our fights and quarrels, so that we can name you Lysimache, the woman who puts a stop to the fighting' (991-2). Since Lysimache is said to have held office for so many decades, she could certainly have been in office both in 421 and 411 BC.

There are other strong parallels between Lysistrata, the heroine of the comedy, and the role of the priestess of Athena Polias at Athens. The priestess had a residence on the acropolis and could not be married: could this be why Lysistrata never seems to speak specifically of a husband, children or household of her own, and is far less sex-obsessed than the other women? The priestess of Athena had the duty of organising the preparation of sacred banquets: Lysistrata invites the Athenian and Spartan negotiators into a ritual meal to ratify their treaty (1181-7). Like the priestess of Athena who, nearly a century before, had stood up to the Spartan invaders, Lysistrata is totally fearless in the face of male violence: she is not afraid of the men attacking the barricaded acropolis (248-51), she wards off the thuggish Scythian sent to arrest her (431-6), and like Athena in a Homeric battle utters the battle-cry to bring the battalions of women out of the acropolis (456-65).

The priestess of Athena also had an unusual degree of public power: unlike other women, she could take men to court and be charged with offences herself. It is interesting, therefore, to find that Lysistrata is named out loud and in public, in front of and by men, without losing any dignity or respectability (1086-7, see also 1103, 1147): citizen women would normally be ashamed to be named in public. Lysistrata is also an expert on weaving, as she shows in the extended metaphor by which she conceives of organising and administering the state as a process of textile production – the weaving of a cloak (667-86). Athena was herself of course the goddess of weaving in her role as Athena *Ergane*, 'Athena of handicrafts'. But even more significantly, weaving was a central duty of the goddess's high priestess. She trained the female teenage attendants who officiated in the cult, including the two specially selected high-born girls who were chosen to live on the acropolis for the nine months leading up to the Panathenaea (the great summer festival of Athena). These two girls, called the *arrephoroi*, had to weave the new gown for the goddess's statue, and to supervise eleven younger girls who helped them in this arduous task. It is significant that the chorus of *Lysistrata* remember fulfilling the role of *arrephoros* in their younger days (638-41).

Lysistrata's command of ritual is very impressive, as would befit the priestess of Athena Polias. She leads the discussion about the correct procedures for conducting the 'sacrifice' (183-97), performs the actual libation to the goddess Persuasion (203-4), leads the oath-taking (209-38), has access to and herself recites the bird oracle (770-6), and orchestrates and directs the hymn-singing at the end, including the Spartan's hymn to 'Spartan' Athena (1273-8, 1295). It is also possible that the selection of the name of one of her chief accomplices, Myrrhine, is a reference to the name of one of the real Lysimache's staff on the acropolis. An epitaph tells us that a woman named Myrrhine was a priestess of Athena Nike, 'Victorious Athena', whose little temple was added to the acropolis' buildings under the Periclean building programme.

There are other references in the play to the cult and rituals of Athena Polias. The third woman who tries to escape from the acropolis has put a helmet under her costume in order to appear pregnant (749-55): this is the helmet associated in art with Athena. We also hear of the owls, Athena's birds, who live on the acropolis but keep the fourth escapee awake at night (760-1). Indeed, if Lysistrata shares many features with Lysimache, the priestess of Athena Polias, by the end of the play her persona seems to merge just as much with the actual goddess herself. In the fantastic version of Athens that we are watching, the heroine can virtually turn into her patron goddess. In a remarkable scene, it transpires that she (alone among the cast of this play) possesses the ability to summon into the theatre an entirely supernatural being, the personification of Reconciliation. By the time the two adversarial sides have agreed to be reconciled with one another, the chorus speaks of Lysistrata in such honorific terms that it is almost as if she has turned into Athena herself (1108-11).

We do not know whether Lysimache, the priestess of Athena, had actually taken it upon herself to complain on behalf of the women of Athens about the devastating losses that were being caused by the long drawn-out Peloponnesian War. It is not at all impossible that she had. The historical situation had become increasingly desperate for the Athenians, who had lost a vast number of their adult citizen males just two years previously on the battlefields and in the quarries of Sicily, as a result of the ill-judged and ill-fated expedition to that island. The losses were so great that there could hardly have been an Athenian family that was not directly affected by a bereavement. This sense certainly lies behind Lysistrata's explanation to the magistrate of the timing of her plot (523-6): we put up with it all for years, she says, but when the time came when we were hearing people saying openly in the street, 'there is no man left in the whole country', we decided that we had to unite to save Greece. What exactly, she asks, were they supposed to wait for?

There also seem to be hints of what the real women of Athens may have been feeling and saying, at least in private, in her account of women's role in war and its impact upon them (587-93): 'We bear war's burden twice over: in the first place by giving birth to our sons and then by sending them out as hoplites ... and then, at the age when we ought to be having fun and enjoying our prime, we have to sleep alone because of the campaigns. About our own position I do not speak, but I am deeply saddened by the number of spinsters growing old in their virginal bedrooms.'

Just how much did the women of Athens complain about their plight? The priestess of Athena would certainly have been a sensible advocate for them to approach. Scholars often point to the passage in Pericles' funeral oration, delivered in honour of the first Peloponnesian War dead in 431 BC, in which he tells the women who have lost men to bear up and not to make a fuss, since 'the greatest glory of a woman is to be mentioned as little as possible' (Thucydides 2.44-5). But why did Pericles feel the need to say this? Is he simply reminding the quiet and docile female population to remain quiet and docile? Or is he actually forced to mention the women because he is faced with a militant, distraught and noisy group of ritual mourners – grandmothers, wives, sisters, daughters – who are going to make life difficult for politicians advocating war? We just do not know. In 431 BC, the women of Athenians may still have kept their complaints behind closed doors, but the situation by two decades later was considerably more catastrophic.

When Aristophanes created his plots and his roles, he had an extraordinarily large repertoire of myth, history, visual art, real life, and theatrical precedent on which he could draw. His *Lysistrata* shares features with the sex-striking epic heroine Alcmena, the Lemnian Hypsipyle, the Queen of the Amazons depicted in Athenian art, and the Wise Melanippe in Euripides' famous lost tragedy. But she also displays numerous features that seem to have been suggested by the office of the high priestess of Athena, and even by the woman who held that office in 411 BC, the aristocratic Lysimache. By the end of the play, in a final twist, she seems almost to turn into Athena herself as she summons the divine personification of Reconciliation and declares that Greece shall put down its weapons. It is to Aristophanes' credit – and to that of the expert cross-dressing actor who may have inspired him to break the hitherto exclusively male mould of the comic hero in writing this brilliant role – that *Lysistrata*'s many faces fuse so well to create such a clearly drawn, heartwarming and memorable personality.

4

Lysistrata the Warrior

Alan H. Sommerstein

Lysistrata is Aristophanes' great peace play, of course. Everyone knows that, even those who know very little else about Aristophanes; the play has been performed countless times as an act of protest against this, that or the other use of military force, from Vietnam to Iraq, and on one day in March 2003 there were twenty-six public readings of the play in the Chicago area alone as part of a worldwide protest action called the Lysistrata Project. In the years 2001-7 inclusive, the Oxford Archive of Performances of Greek and Roman Drama records 44 productions of *Lysistrata* (or adaptations thereof) in all countries, nearly three times as many as for any other Aristophanic play and more than for the three old favourites, *Birds*, *Frogs* and *Clouds*, put together; and of course that means a good many more than 44 actual performances. And while the play's sexual theme no doubt accounts for some part of this popularity, it is likely to have been of very secondary significance; *Ecclesiazusae*, which also has a sexual theme, received just six productions. *Lysistrata* is a hit because it is thought of – along with that very different work, Euripides' *Trojan Women* – as *the* anti-war drama of antiquity, and its author – in the words of his finest present-day French interpreter, Pascal Thiercy – as 'le grand poète pacifiste'.

What I am going to argue here is that this has very little to do with anything in *Lysistrata* itself. I have no idea what Lysistrata's attitude, or Aristophanes', would have been to modern conflicts fought in a world whose politics, and whose technology, they could never have imagined in their wildest fantasies.

But neither of them can reasonably be regarded as an unconditional opponent of war and violence *under all circumstances* (which is what I take 'pacifist' to mean), or even as an unconditional advocate of ending the current war against Sparta.

To begin with the weaker claim. Well, for a start, Lysistrata herself is quite prepared to order the actual use of violence, as when she gives military orders to 'four ... companies of fully armed fighting women' (453-4) to attack the Scythian archers who are attempting to arrest her and her leading followers. And even her famous tactic of a sex-strike is no mere withdrawal of labour; it is presented as making itself effective through the infliction on the men of severe physical pain (845, 967, 1089-90) which is explicitly compared to the pain of someone undergoing one of the worse forms of torture (846). That enforced abstinence from sex (or rather from *marital* sex, this being the only kind over which the strikers have any control) could have such an effect is of course a comic absurdity; the fact remains that in the play it *does* have this effect, and it is Lysistrata's intention that it should. She is as much applying physical coercion to the men as if she had led a besieging army to blockade and starve them, or as if she had sprayed their eyes with some non-lethal but painful chemical (that's not being anachronistic; it's suggested, as a tactic for naval warfare, by Euripides in the *Frogs*).

However, 'that singular anomaly the violent pacifist' (to re-adapt a line of W.S. Gilbert's *Mikado* that has been adapted dozens of times before) is a figure that we are all familiar with and for whom we are usually prepared to make allowances; and there is certainly a big difference between the kinds of violence Lysistrata practises, which are never going to be fatal to anyone, and the kinds routinely practised in actual warfare. But then it turns out that Lysistrata isn't a straightforward hater of actual warfare, either.

Of course the women are consistently and passionately eager for the current war against Sparta to be brought to an end. There are, however, a considerable number of references in the play to military actions conducted in the past, or anticipated in the future, by the Athenian people and/or their allies against opponents *other* than Sparta. And *every one of these references is a favourable one*. And I am not talking here about remarks made by the bellicose (and often stupid) male characters who deride and resist the heroine and her supporters. I am talking about things that are said by Lysistrata herself, by her confederates, and later by Athenian and Spartan men who have accepted her demands and agreed to make peace with each other.

Most of these references are to past, or prospective, wars against Persia. To be sure, the Persian War of 480-479 was a defensive one, and it is likely, though it is not made explicit, that the future war against Persia envisaged in line 1133 is being thought of as defensive too. But to a genuine pacifist, that should be neither here nor there; and in any case the *first* time the women mention the Persian War, at 653, it is not as a patriotic struggle for independence but as a source of material gain, as having enabled Athens to enrich herself (probably referring to the tribute paid by her allies, many of whom had previously been paying it to the Persians). Later, too, when one of the Spartan men offers to sing a song 'in honour of both the Athenians and ourselves', one might have expected him to choose a subject appropriate to the mood of the moment, which is one of convivial celebration; and he does indeed end (1262-72) by calling on Artemis to bless the newly-made peace treaty 'with everlasting friendship and prosperity' – but up to that point his song has been about battle, about Athens' victory (rather generously so called) at Artemisium and Spartan heroism at Thermopylae.

Before that, in the course of her successful attempt to persuade the Athenians and Spartans to end their conflict, Lysistrata mentions other good services that the two cities had performed for each other in the past, for which each of them (she says) ought to feel gratitude and act accordingly. And each time, the service she recalls is a military one; and more than that, each time Lysistrata edits history to make the service more altruistic and/or more effective than in fact it was. The Athenian service to Sparta is Cimon's expedition in 462 to assist Sparta against the Messenians at Ithome (1138-44), which according to Lysistrata 'saved all Lacedaemon'; in fact, even supposing (which is doubtful) that Sparta was still seriously threatened at that stage, Cimon *failed* to capture the

39

rebel stronghold, and shortly thereafter the Spartans sent his army home in circumstances that made the whole affair a humiliation for Athens and especially for Cimon, who was ostracised at the next opportunity. The Spartan service to Athens was her military intervention in 510 to impose a regime change by overthrowing the tyrant Hippias; it is not mentioned that Sparta hoped and expected that this would lead to the installation of a friendly aristocratic regime, and that, when Cleisthenes established a democracy instead, Sparta intervened again to prevent this. Twice over, that is, Lysistrata twists and spins the facts to whitewash a military action of dubious motive or consequence.

This attitude of Lysistrata's is not in the least abnormal, for Aristophanes. There is no passage in any of his surviving plays in which any character expresses opposition to any past, present or prospective war against any opponent other than Sparta – *unless* that war either (i) has already ended in obvious failure or (ii) is being used as a stick with which to beat a politician whom the dramatist detests anyway for other reasons. The Sicilian expedition nicely illustrates both the exception and the rule. In *Lysistrata* it is recalled as an utter disaster; the decision to launch it was attended by evil omens, the politician who advocated it is cursed (391-7), and when Lysistrata mentions the suffering of mothers who sent their sons to fight as hoplites (589-590) – she would have said 'never to see them again', and the Proboulos hastily interrupts her, but all he can say is 'be quiet', because he has no counter-argument. But that is in *Lysistrata*, after it's all over. In *Birds*, when it is still in progress and the prospects look good, the only complaint anyone makes about the campaign is that Nicias is taking too long to win it (639). Elsewhere, not only the Persian War but sundry campaigns of imperial enforcement, at Naxos or Byzantium or on Euboea, are mentioned with pride, and Melos, scene of a massacre that was remembered as a stain on Athens' name for generations, becomes material for a cheery joke (*Birds* 186).

The other type of exception that I mentioned can be illustrated by the case of Hyperbolus in the second parabasis of *Knights* (1300-15). It was alleged – with what measure of truth, we have no idea – that at this time (425/4 BC) Hyperbolus was advocating a large naval expedition against Carthage, and the ships of the fleet are represented as being appalled by this proposal and ready to go to considerable lengths to frustrate it. What Aristophanes' opinion was about the political or strategic merits of such a scheme in the abstract, we cannot tell; what we *can* say is that he always expresses hostility to *anything* that he associates with the name of Hyperbolus. It has often been observed, indeed, that he likes to wind up a list of blessings by adding ' ... and getting rid of Hyperbolus' or words to that effect. So if Hyperbolus was the principal advocate of a particular campaign, Aristophanes (and most other comic dramatists, for that matter) could be guaranteed to be against it. That shows that they disliked Hyperbolus (or wanted to be perceived as disliking him); it shows nothing about their attitude to war.

Even if we confine our consideration to the war against Sparta, Lysistrata's strategy is decidedly hard-headed. Not for her the approach of the so-called peace women of Greenham Common, with whom she and her followers were famously compared by Tony Harrison in his play *The Common Chorus*; there is no thought of unilateral disarmament or unilateral concession. Instead, she takes no action until she has secured the agreement of women in the enemy states to take corresponding action, and even after they have not merely agreed but sworn to do so, she still does not trust them completely and takes all but one of their representatives as hostages (244) – while surrendering none herself. Clearly she is not seeking peace at any price. Can we say, at least symbolically, what her price actually is?

Well, before the peace treaty is finally agreed there is a short bout of negotiation between the leaders of the Athenian and Spartan delegations (1161-72). Now the negotiations are not designed for one moment to be thought of as a serious piece of diplomacy; the two sides' territorial claims are mapped out on the naked (or pseudo-naked) body of a personified feminine abstraction named Reconciliation, and the particular places mentioned are chosen for the sake of a series of ingenious and hilarious anatomical double entendres. Nevertheless, the scales of advantage are decidedly tilted. The Spartan makes the first demand, for Pylos (1164). The Athenian protests, but Lysistrata tells him to hand it over and 'ask for another place in return for that one'. He goes considerably further; he asks for *three* places – Echinus, the Malian Gulf, and the Long Walls of Megara (here called the Megarian Legs). Not surprisingly, the Spartan demurs. And what does Lysistrata do? She just says 'Let it be – don't go quarrelling about a pair of legs' (1172) – and that is the end of the negotiations. That last response of Lysistrata's has its verbs in the singular, not the plural, so it is addressed to only one of the two sides; I would have thought it obvious that it is the Spartan (the last previous speaker) who is being told to concede, but at least one astute scholar, the late Antonio López Eire (in a Spanish translation of 1994), has taken it the other way, so for the sake of argument I will accept that view. In that case, the Athenians are told to drop the third of their three demands, but they are given the other two, so they gain twice as much from the negotiations as the Spartans do; what is more, the place that is 'given' to the Spartans, Pylos in Messenia, had been Spartan territory for three hundred years until captured by Cleon and Demosthenes in 425, whereas Echinus and the Malian Gulf had never been under Athenian control and they had held the Megarian Long Walls only for two short periods. That is from the geographical point of view. From the anatomical point of view, as all recent commentators observe, the Athenians are getting exactly what they desire, since their demand is for Reconciliation's vulva (and the surrounding district) while the Spartans, in accordance with the Athenian stereotype of Spartan sexual proclivities, want her anus; so that in the end both are satisfied (and say so, this time in agricultural language, in 1173-4) – but the Athenians will certainly feel that they have made the better bargain.

In other words, the peace Lysistrata makes, while both sides accept it, is a peace that gives more advantages to Athens than to Sparta. That was certainly not the kind of peace that anyone could remotely envisage as possible in the real world early in 411, little over a year after the Sicilian disaster. Not long afterwards, Peisander was trying to persuade the Assembly to recall Alcibiades from exile, negotiate an alliance with Persia and, if necessary, make major constitutional changes at Athens in order to get it. When he met fierce opposition on political and religious grounds, he challenged his opponents to explain 'what possible hope of safety they had for the city' if his plan was not followed; none of them could find an answer (Thucydides 8.53.2-3). Not too long after that, when the Four Hundred had come to power (but without a Persian alliance, and without Alcibiades), Peisander discovered, not with pleasure, how right he had been, when the new regime sought to open negotiations with Sparta. Their first attempt came to nothing; sending an embassy to King Agis at Deceleia, they proposed peace on the basis of the *status quo*, but Agis replied that Athens' maritime empire must be disbanded. The negotiations broke down, and Agis marched on Athens, expecting to take it without a fight; on meeting resistance, he retreated, and began to encourage the Four Hundred to send a delegation to Sparta itself (Thucydides 8.70.2-71.3). It seems to have been some time before they actually did so, and when they did they made the blunder of sending it on a state trireme with a strongly democratic crew; the delegation ended up in prison at Argos (Thucydides 8.86.9). Eventually, fearing (not without reason) that their fall was imminent, the Four Hundred sent a new, high-powered delegation post-haste to Sparta with instructions 'at all costs to make any terms with the Spartans that were in any way endurable'. According to Thucydides they had three negotiating positions: first, the terms that Agis had originally rejected, with Athens allowed to retain control of its allies; secondly, if this was refused, at least for Athens to be independent and retain its walls and fleet; and thirdly, if even that failed, they were willing to accept any terms at all, even including a Spartan occupation of Athens, if only they could save their own skins. They came home 'having secured no agreement for everyone', which strongly suggests, as Donald Kagan has argued (*The Fall of the Athenian Empire*, 192), that they *had* secured an agreement for themselves – in other words, the third option (Thucydides 8.90.2-91.3). But it was too late, both for them and for the Spartans, and they were overthrown by internal resistance.

That final fiasco doesn't in itself prove that the Spartans might not have made a better offer at an earlier stage; by the time of the final negotiations they must have felt that they would probably in any case be in control of Athens, directly or indirectly, within the month. But it is surely unimaginable that *before* the takeover by the Four Hundred, with Athens still democratic and Sparta believing it had the stronger navy and the prospect of Persian support, there would have been any chance at all of Sparta agreeing to a peace under which Athens would retain her maritime empire. And that, we may be sure, was the only peace that most Athenians would have been prepared to countenance; we may be sure of that because initially even the oligarchs, when this proposal was rejected by Agis, did not put forward their later Plan B (let alone Plan C) but simply withdrew from the negotiations. They knew that if they came back and said, 'We've been offered peace on condition that we give up the empire, and we're going to accept the offer', they wouldn't last a week. But that was the best offer they were likely to get. And a democratic Athens would be very lucky indeed even to get that much – unless and until it managed to change the odds by gaining a naval victory or two.

Lysistrata's peace was thus a fantasy, and everyone knew it. Indeed, this is admitted within the play itself. After the two hostile choruses of men and women are reconciled and combine into one, they make a series of Magnificent Free Offers to the audience (1043-71, 1188-1215) each of which is neatly nullified in the small print: you're all invited to dinner – but my front door will be shut; if your children are taking part in a procession, I'm happy for you to borrow all the fancy clothing and jewellery I own – only I don't own any; my servant has been ordered to hand out sacks of grain to all comers – but if you come anywhere near my door, beware of the dog! Those are the second, third and fourth of the offers. The first one, translated into the terms of modern advertising, might come out something like this.

> Are you stuck for a spot of cash? Two or three hundred drachmas, say? Then come round to our place and just pick it up – and get a purse to put it in, absolutely free! (Terms and conditions apply. If peace ever comes, repayment of principal will not be required.)

What sounded like a gift has turned out to be a loan, and an interest-bearing loan at that. It does seem to have one redeeming feature: the debt will be cancelled 'if peace ever comes'. But remember, these offers are all meant to be, in the end, worthless. The presupposition must therefore be that peace will either never come at all, or will take so long that by that time the lender will have got his money back, perhaps several times over, in the form of interest (rate not stated, but even a respectable banker might charge 36% on high-risk loans: Lysias, fragment 1). That is the chorus's, and the audience's, actual expectation, once they leave the theatre.

The objective of the play, therefore, is emphatically not to encourage the Athenians to take political or other action aimed at ending the war. The prospect of such action being successful was, and was known to be, not measurably different from zero. Unless, that is, you were a supporter of oligarchy, and hoped or expected, as the Four Hundred did, that the Spartans would offer better terms to an oligarchic regime than to 'the untrustworthy *demos*' (Thucydides 8.70.2); but whatever may have been Aristophanes' actual views on *that* subject, he never expresses explicitly anti-democratic sentiments, or allows any sympathetic character to do so, in this play or in any other, and indeed all but makes Lysistrata claim (falsely), in commendation of the Spartans, that they were responsible for the creation of Athenian democracy in the first place (1156). Rather, as is often the case in Old Comedy, the objective is to transport the audience into a dream world, where benevolent gods aid a determined human hero (or, as in this case, heroine) to rescue Athens or Greece or humanity from a perilous predicament.

The gods, or rather goddesses, who aid Lysistrata's campaign are three in number. The first, and least important, is Artemis, who is of course among other things a goddess of chastity. Of the four women (if it is four) who confront the Proboulos in lines 435-48, two swear their defiance by Artemis (435, 447) and a third by Hecate (Phosphoros) who is sometimes identified with her (443); in her celebrated non-seduction scene with Cinesias, Myrrhine too swears twice by Artemis (922, 949); the Spartan's song celebrating the Persian War and the new peace treaty ends with a prayer to Artemis Agrotera (1262-72), and a subsequent cletic (invocation) hymn, probably sung by Lysistrata herself, summons Artemis first among the major deities (1280);

in addition, we are reminded indirectly of Artemis twice, once when the women are compared to Artemisia, the queen of Halicarnassus who fought at Salamis (675), and once when the Spartan sings of the battle of Artemisium (1251).

Secondly, and not surprisingly, Aphrodite, whose power is invoked at three crucial moments. Lysistrata begins her main speech in the *agon* (551-2) by expressing her confidence that the women will triumph 'so long as sweet-souled Eros and Cyprus-born Aphrodite breathe desire over our bosoms and our thighs', and the first cry of support she receives from another woman is an oath in the name of 'Paphian Aphrodite' (556); the first sight of a man in distress owing to the sex-strike (or, as Lysistrata puts it, 'crazed and possessed by the secret rites of Aphrodite' (832) (rites which, as he later reminds his wife (898), she has not practised for a long time) causes her to pray to the 'mistress of Cyprus and Cythera and Paphos' (833-4); and in the final cletic hymn, while all the gods are invited to *witness* the new-made peace, it is Aphrodite who is credited with actually *making* it (1290). And elsewhere, the women swear by Aphrodite in six passages scattered through the play (208, 252, 556, 749, 858, 939).

But the goddess who truly dominates this play, as everyone familiar with it knows, is Athena. When the setting is established (at about line 240), it is the west front of Athena's citadel, the Acropolis, and there is special mention of features like the Nike bastion (317) and the Promachos statue (751ff.). In and around the *parodos* alone, the goddess is mentioned eight times, notably when the Acropolis is occupied (241) and when the women's chorus come to repel the men's attack on it (341-9); and she is also prominent in the Spartan song that concludes the play (at least as we have it), in her Spartan guise as Athena Chalkioikos (1299, 1320-1). Most importantly of all, perhaps, as David Lewis first saw (*Annual of the British School at Athens* 50 [1955] 1-12), the heroine herself has a name, and to some extent a role, reminiscent of Lysimache, the current priestess of Athena Polias (see also in this volume Edith Hall, pp. 32f., James Robson, p. 52 and Martin Revermann, p. 74), to whom she explicitly compares herself and her followers at the beginning of her *agon* speech (554); and I have argued elsewhere (on pp. 302-3 of the addenda to my 2001 edition of *Wealth*) that at the end of the play she is assimilated more closely to Athena herself and may even – as the priestess sometimes did – wear the goddess's distinctive garment, the aegis. This helps to explain why the gods summoned in the cletic hymn 1279-90 include Artemis and Apollo, Dionysus, Zeus and Hera, and by implication Aphrodite, but not Athena: because Athena is already there.

Athena can be a reconciler and unifier (as she is famously in Aeschylus' *Eumenides*), but she is also, especially at Athens, a warrior goddess – indeed *the* warrior goddess – and this is certainly not forgotten in the play. Indeed in the text as we have it the very last word is *pammakhon* 'able to fight any foe', as an epithet of Athena, and while it is likely that this word is not in its correct place (in its present position it plays havoc with the metre), it almost certainly still belongs in the final line. And it should be remembered, too, that while the name of her priestess, Lysimache, can reasonably be read as 'she who resolves strife' (and is, indeed, so read in Aristophanes' earlier play, *Peace* [992], as well as in this one), the actual name of the heroine, Lysistrate, would probably in the normal run of things be understood as meaning not 'she who *disbands* armies', i.e. the peacemaker, but 'she who *scatters* armies', i.e. puts enemies to flight – with a recollection of one of Athena's own epithets, *Phobesistrate* 'she who *routs* armies'.

Of course Athenians in 411 wanted the war to end. But as we have seen, most of them still regarded as unthinkable any terms for ending it that did not preserve their right to control, and raise revenue from, the states in their alliance; and since many of these states had already *de facto* seceded (though some had since been reconquered), the very bottom line of acceptability would be the *status quo* – which, as we have also seen, there was no chance of their being offered. (They *were* offered it in 410, after their crushing naval victory at Cyzicus – and they rejected it: Diodorus Siculus 13.52-3.)

Lysistrata does considerably better. She coerces the Athenian males, but she also arranges for the coercion of the Spartan males; and as the Spartan Lampito had envisaged from the start (168-71), it is in fact the Spartans who crack first. After the long scene in which Cinesias is tantalised and tormented by his wife, he still does not say he is ready to make peace, and it is the Spartans who make the first approach to seek a settlement. During Lysistrata's speech to the two delegations, both leaders are repeatedly distracted by the beauty of Reconciliation, but it is only the Spartan who is so far gone as to admit that his city is in the wrong (1148). And as we have seen, in the arguments over territorial issues the Athenians get the better of it – perhaps by a wider margin than I have cautiously assumed. Lysistrata in that final scene is usually, and rightly, thought of as a neutral figure above the conflict. But she is certainly, from an Athenian point of view, the right kind of neutral. How could she not be? She is Athenian herself, and she also represents the goddess who was Athens' very own, even if she *was* also worshipped at Sparta. And the peace that she creates is a peace that most Athenians, in the circumstances of 411, would be more than happy with, a peace *better* than they could have gained by normal diplomatic means. It is also a pipe dream.

I am not saying that Aristophanes the man did not strongly desire an end to the war with Sparta – probably a good deal more strongly than most of his fellow-citizens, to judge from the strong contrast between his approach to wars against Sparta and his approach to all other wars. Nor am I saying that Aristophanes the dramatist was not to some extent hoping to persuade his audience to take a similar view. All I am saying is that he neither believed, nor wished his audience to believe, that war was invariably, or even usually, a terrible evil to be avoided at all costs, and that even when Sparta was the enemy, nothing in any of his plays suggests that he would have accepted a peace that did not leave Athens free to maintain her empire and indeed, where there was a good prospect of success, to expand it. And what is true for him is also true for his creation, Lysistrata: neither of them ever forgets that it takes two to make a peace.

This essay appeared previously, in a slightly different form, in A.H. Sommerstein, *Talking about Laughter and Other Studies in Greek Comedy* (Oxford: Oxford University Press, 2009) 223-36.

Friends and Foes:
The People of *Lysistrata*

James Robson

In a play where battle lines are drawn up from the very beginning, it matters who you are in *Lysistrata*. The play was first
staged in 411 BC against the backdrop of a war raging between
Athens and Sparta – and, as in the real world, nationality plays
a key role in dictating the characters' allegiances. But it is, of
course, on a very different basis that the lines of conflict are
drawn up at the beginning of *Lysistrata*: gender. So, men are
pitched against women in the play – although not, perhaps, in a
wholly predictable way. The battle is, in fact, fought on two very
different fronts, the sparring choruses of old men and old
women forming a counterpoint to the conflict between the
younger women (led by Lysistrata) and the various male visitors that arrive at the occupied Acropolis.

In this essay, I shall explore the ways in which different
social groups found in *Lysistrata* are presented: not only groups
central to the action like old men, old women, younger women
and Spartans, but also those given less attention in the play,
such as Athens' slaves and immigrants. As we shall see, Aristophanes' characterisation of the people of *Lysistrata* is always
carefully managed and not without its surprises.

Old men and old women

The choruses of old men and old women play an interesting role
in Lysistrata, not least because their behaviour so often prefig-
ures that of the younger characters. The *parodos* (the entry of

the choruses following the prologue), for example, is the first glimpse we get of men and women in direct conflict, and towards the end of the play it is the choruses who are the first to reconcile their differences. These chorus members are characterised quite distinctly from the younger characters, however. Arguably, both the older men and the women are more physically combative than their younger counterparts and both are prone to reflect on past glories. For example, both groups claim to have served the city well in their various ways: the old men as fighters at battles such as Marathon (285), the old women as active participants in the city's religious institutions and festivals (638-47). The two groups could, then, be said to have crucial qualities in common – first, an instinct to fight, and second, a common history and purpose – which makes their early reconciliation all the more credible.

This *parodos* scene, where we first meet the rival choruses, is carefully plotted by Aristophanes. No sooner have we been informed by Lysistrata of the plan to occupy the Acropolis (240-2) than the old men arrive, vowing to 'consign to flame all the women who have instigated and pursued this plan' (268-9). An ancient audience, expecting a full chorus of twenty-four members, might have been surprised at the appearance of a semi-chorus of just twelve old men, but they would not have had long to wait until the arrival of the twelve members of the women's semi-chorus who come with water to thwart the men's plans (319). This splitting of the chorus into two distinct groups neatly reinforces the theme of division in the early part of the play (just as its subsequent unification helps to underline the theme of reconciliation later on). We might remark, too, that the men's carrying of wood and the women's carrying of pitchers reflect typical domestic duties of the two sexes for lower-class Athenians and therefore act as clear visual indicators for an audience of the choruses' gender and status.

Fire and water are strong symbols exploited by Aristophanes to full effect in this scene (and indeed throughout the play). For example, the older men's fire mirrors the fiery passion of the younger men later in the play, which the older women with their water are easily able to quench when they choose, just as the younger women would be able, when *they* choose, to quench their husbands' passion. There is also, surely, sexual symbolism in the phallic logs carried by the men which contrast with the women's pitchers. Indeed, the theme of the sex-strike is brilliantly underscored by another instance of sexual imagery: the men's attempts to use the logs as a battering ram against the closed gate of the Acropolis (the Propylaea: 308-9).

The way in which the two groups handle their chosen weapons also adds to their characterisation. The old men find carrying the wood difficult and, when lighting the fire, they temporarily blind themselves with the smoke (295). The old women on the other hand encounter no such difficulties with their pitchers, which they nimbly manoeuvre to drench the men with water (381-4). Put simply, the women outwit the men with their superior speed and organisation.

Towards the end of the play it is the old women who are the peace brokers: they are the first to make moves towards reconciliation in the choral exchange which follows the Cinesias and Myrrhine scene (1014-42). The women's leader offers to be a 'firm friend' to the men's leader (1017), despite the men's continuing hostility, and she then shows her care by clothing him (1021) and taking out the gnat that is in his eye (1031-2). This is a particularly neat touch by Aristophanes since this action symbolically restores the men's sight: now that the men can see clearly, they are content to make peace!

Women in a man's world

Women in Old Comedy tend to share two character traits: they are sex-mad and overfond of alcohol. Given the first of these traits, a sex-strike instigated by a woman is a particularly strong idea for a comedy, since Aristophanes is able to make great humorous capital from the fact that the women first reject the idea of the strike altogether (124-39) and later appear to weaken in their resolve (we encounter a series of lame excuses as various women try to sneak out of the Acropolis: 718-67). Women's supposed keenness for alcohol is given far less prominence in this play, although this trait does briefly become the source of some choice humour during the oath-swearing scene, where the 'slaughter' of a jar of Thasian wine

– presided over by Lysistrata – stands in place of an animal sacrifice (194-7), and the other women then compete to be the first to drink (207-8).

Lysistrata is carefully characterised as different from the other Athenian women. In contrast to them, nothing she says indicates any weakness for sex, alcohol, or indeed, any hint of frivolity at all. She also gains status in the play by being cast as something of a priestess figure. There are various indications of this: her first lines in the play, for example, are an allusion to religious festivals (1-4) and we have already seen the way she presides over the 'sacrifice' of the jar of wine. Perhaps most significant, however, is the fact that one of the most important priestesses in Athens at that time (the priestess of Athena Polias – 'Athena protectress of the city' – whose precinct lay on the Acropolis) was called Lysimache, 'Dissolver of Battles' (cf. Lysistrata, 'Dissolver of Armies'; see also in this volume Martin Revermann, p. 74, Edith Hall, pp. 32f. and Alan Sommerstein, p. 46). Characterising Lysistrata in this way has two advantages for Aristophanes. First, he at once endows Lysistrata with the kind of authority a woman would need to organise other women and to command the respect of men, making her leadership appear all the more natural. Second, it allows him subtly to evoke the one occasion on which women could collect together outside their homes without men being present, namely a religious festival – so the female gathering at the beginning of the play seems less forced than it might otherwise.

In the prologue, various Athenian women outline the difficulties they have in leaving the house undetected by their husbands, underlining the fact that they are essentially housewives. This 'housewifeyness' is important to the play, as one of the striking elements of *Lysistrata* is the way in which concepts are taken from the female, domestic sphere and are brought to bear on the broader world of the *polis* (city-state). Notable examples of this include Lysistrata's suggestion that women's expertise in the management of household finances can be successfully applied to the city as a whole (493-5) and the women's dressing up of the Magistrate (*Proboulos*) as a corpse (reflecting women's extensive role in burial: 599-613). The most striking instance, though, is surely Lysistrata's solution to the city's problems, which she presents in terms of a metaphor of wool-working (567-86: discussed more fully below).

Aristophanes treads an interesting line, then, in his creation of female figures in this play, blending accurate detail of women's everyday lives with popular comic stereotypes. And this interweaving of the realistic and the absurd is, to a large extent, a characteristic of the play as a whole. After all, one vital point to bear in mind is that the premise underpinning the plot of *Lysistrata* is essentially fantastic. A scenario in which women gather together in secret, where they plot and fight against men and take charge of the city's affairs (albeit temporarily) was unthinkable in the real world of fifth-century Athens. Aristophanes is constantly playing with the topsy-turvy idea of women in power to great effect and much of the appeal of the wool-working metaphor, for instance, comes from the way in which he takes this domestic image from the woman's realm and cleverly applies it to the male, public domain. In so doing, Aristophanes almost makes the concept of female rule seem logical, whereas to his audience the idea of women running the city would have been quite ridiculous: a concept suitable to myth, fantasy or even barbarian societies, but not to real life in a Greek *polis*.

Athens and Sparta

In 411 BC, the year of *Lysistrata*'s production, the Peloponnesian War was in a position of stalemate. Disaster had loomed for the Athenians in 413 BC after their catastrophic campaign in Sicily, but while the odds were still stacked in the Spartans' favour, some minor Athenian naval victories and even the regaining by Athens of some previously lost territory indicated that the city was still a force to be reckoned with. The real-life war is absorbed by Aristophanes into the fictional world of *Lysistrata* and provides the backdrop to – and indeed the motivation for – the women's sex-strike.

Given that *Lysistrata* was performed in Athens some twenty years after the initial outbreak of war with Sparta (and needless to say, to an audience that would have been nothing if not partisan), perhaps the single most remarkable feature of *Lysis-*

trata is the positive press it gives to the Spartans. To take a simple example, in a pause in the celebrations that end the play, an Athenian remarks 'the Spartans really were so charming!' (1226) and it is noteworthy that in a play which celebrates peace, it is the Spartans who are the more eager to end the war. It is the Spartans, too, who send an embassy to Athens, rather than the other way round (980ff. and 1072ff.) – hardly a reflection of real life in 411 BC, since it was the Spartans who had the upper hand in the fighting. All this stands in stark contrast, too, to Aristophanes' portrayal of Athens and the Athenians which is far from complimentary!

So, does Aristophanes portray the Spartans simply as charming peacemakers? Not quite. At lines 628-9, the chorus of old men claims that 'men of Laconia ... can be no more trusted than a ravening wolf', a comment which reflects the reputation Spartans had in antiquity for being deceitful. This quality is mentioned again later (1269-70), when the Spartan sings 'may we be rid of all wily foxes': that is to say, may we cease being deceitful. What is more, the Spartans are the first to admit to Lysistrata 'We're in the wrong' in connection with the war (1147). But even these points can be made to seem positive, I think. Perhaps the old men's chorus is to be seen as unsympathetic and as voicing an unreasonable prejudice, looking for reasons to prolong the war. Perhaps the Spartan's open admission of wiliness can be taken as actually signalling the opposite of wiliness opposite, namely honesty. Perhaps the Spartans' admission of wrongdoing can be taken as a willingness to compromise – a conciliatory step to make it easier for the Athenians to make peace.

A particularly fascinating take on the question of Aristophanes' depiction of Sparta comes from an analysis of the way in which historical events are presented in the play. Lysistrata's memory is long and one of the events she mentions during the reconciliation scene is the expulsion of the tyrant Hippias from Athens in 510 BC. This account she gives of the end of Hippias' tyranny (1150-6), in which she attributes a decisive role in the liberation of Athens to King Cleomenes of Sparta, is nothing short of extraordinary. After all, few Athenians would have thought to mention the role of Cleomenes in these events – rather, popular wisdom was that the tyranny effectively ended when Hippias' brother Hipparchus was slain by two Athenian lovers, Harmodius and Aristogeiton in 514 BC (Thucydides confirms this popular view of events in his *History of the Peloponnesian War* (1.20) and these events also formed the subject of a number of popular drinking songs).

Another curious description given by Lysistrata is of the mission led by the Athenian Cimon, sent to help the Spartans after the earthquake of 464 BC and the subsequent revolt of Sparta's serf population, the helots. Her version of events (1138-44) describes a desperate Sparta saved from near disaster by Athens' timely help. In actual fact, Cimon's help was ignominiously rejected by Sparta (possibly because the democratic sensibilities of the Athenian troops led them to sympathise with the helots) and the whole debacle led to his enforced exile from Athens. There is no hint of this in Lysistrata's revisionist account.

The way history is presented would, then, seem to promote a view of profitable co-operation between Athens and Sparta – a theme which is picked up by the Spartan's song about the Persian Wars towards the end of the play (1248-72), where both sides' achievements in the Greek victory over the Persians nearly 70 years before are given equal weight and where prayers are made for lasting unity between the two cities. The one instance of a Spartan hostile to Athens comes at lines 274-80 where, as I have mentioned, the (unsympathetic?) old men's chorus makes mention of King Cleomenes' occupation of the Acropolis in 508 BC – but, of course, this is the same Cleomenes who is later credited with helping to put an end to the tyranny. Once again, then, an unfavourable swipe against the Spartans by the old men's chorus can be thought of as revisited and trumped by a positive image later in the play.

There are further ways, too, in which Sparta is given a positive spin in *Lysistrata*. The city was famed for the beauty of its women (Helen of Troy was a Spartan), and this positive stereotype appears to be freely drawn on by Aristophanes in his characterisation of Lampito, the one Spartan female we meet in the play. When she arrives at the women's meeting, she is addressed by Lysistrata in the following terms (78-81):

Welcome, Lampito, my very dear Laconian friend! Darling, what
beauty you display! What a fine colour, and what a robust frame
you've got! You could throttle a bull.

To which Calonice adds (83):

What a splendid pair of tits you've got!

So, Lampito is beautiful, physically fit and, perhaps, has her
breasts on display (Spartan women supposedly exercised in the
nude). This praise of Spartan women is picked up later in the
song which ends our text of the play, where they are said to
dance 'like fillies, raising clouds of dust with their feet' beside
the River Eurotas (1308-11). Is it fair to claim that Aristophanes has chosen to emphasise a particularly attractive feature of Spartan civilisation to his male spectators – its women?
Spartans were also much celebrated for their achievements in
the area of song and dance and a good part of the celebrations
at the end of the play are taken up by these activities (there is
even a song about the glory of Sparta: 1296-1315). Again, can
we go as far as to claim that Aristophanes is reminding his
Athenian audience here of high points of Spartan culture?

A final interesting take on Aristophanes' presentation of the
Spartans comes from looking at the Greek they speak in the
play. The Spartan dialect differed from Athenian Greek just as
many dialects of English differ from one another: that is, there
were key differences in both pronunciation and vocabulary.
Here, then, there was an opportunity for Aristophanes to mock
the Spartans, perhaps by making them appear incomprehensi-
ble, stupid or unsophisticated because of their different use of
language. An analysis of his Spartans' Greek, however, shows
nothing of the kind: rather, Aristophanes seems to have made
efforts faithfully to capture the pronunciation and vocabulary of
the Spartan dialect.

Taking all this data together, it is no doubt tempting to
assert, as many scholars have, that Aristophanes is champion-
ing a pro-Spartan, Panhellenic viewpoint in this play (a subject
pursued more fully by Lorna Hardwick in her essay, *Lysistratas
on the Modern Stage*). At this juncture, however, it is perhaps
worth making one point explicit, namely that while Aristo-

phanes as the author of the play is, of course, responsible for its themes and the sentiments expressed by its characters this is not the same as claiming that every opinion, whichever character espouses it, in whatever context, is necessarily that of Aristophanes. There may be all kinds of reasons why an author might (consciously or unconsciously) have his characters state opinions contrary to his or her own. This said, Aristophanes' portrayal of Spartans is certainly striking in this play – especially given the historical context of its first performance.

Other social groups: slaves, immigrants and would-be citizens

So far in this essay we have met a number of paired groups (old men/old women, men/women, Athenians/Spartans), all of which are in conflict at the start of the play but which are reconciled by the play's end. Not all groupings fall neatly into this pattern, however. Perhaps the most noteworthy exception is slaves, a number of whom appear in the play (e.g. the slave girl mentioned in the prologue at line 184 and Cinesias' male childminder, 908). It is interesting that, in contrast with other plays of Aristophanes', slaves play only minor roles in *Lysistrata* and there is no hint of them enjoying the material benefits of peace at the end of the play – on the contrary, some Spartan slaves are actually threatened with being burnt alive (1217-18). Here, then, a further significant pair of groups emerges: those who benefit from the peace (comprising citizens and their wives) and those who do not (namely slaves).

What this new division ignores, however, is a number of potential spectators of *Lysistrata* who fail to fit neatly into the citizen/slave divide. Aristophanes is not unaware of these neglected sections of Athenian society, though, as is evidenced by Lysistrata's much discussed wool-working speech, where she offers what appears to be a programme for political reform (568-70; 574-86):

> It's like when we have a tangled skein of wool. We take it, like this, and pull it gently with the help of our spindles, now this way and now that. That's how we'll unravel this war, if we're

allowed to, sorting it out by sending embassies, now this way and
now that.

...

First of all, just like washing out a raw fleece, you should wash
the sheep-dung out of the body politic in a bath, then put it on a
bed, beat out the villains with a stick and pick off the burrs; and
as for those people who combine and mat themselves together to
gain office, you should card them out and pluck off the heads.
Then card the wool into the work-basket of union and concord,
mixing in everyone; and the immigrants, and any foreigner
who's friendly to you, and anyone in debt to the treasury, they
should be mixed in as well. And yes, there are also all the states
which are colonies of this land: you should recognise how you
now have them lying around like little flocks of wool, each one by
itself; so then you should take the human flock from all of them,
bring them together here and join them into one, and then make
a great ball of wool, and from that weave a warm cloak for the
people to wear.

In this speech, then, Lysistrata likens solving the city's problems to untangling a skein of wool. First, her metaphor leads
her to suggest sending embassies 'now this way and now that'
(570), presumably to sue for peace. She then suggests that
'villains' and 'those people who combine and mat themselves
together to gain office' should be removed from the citizen body:
here the target seems to be public figures who belong to political factions and who conspire to gain money and power. Next
she mentions groups who, she says, should be included in the
citizenry but are currently excluded. Four groups are mentioned: (i) resident immigrants ('metics'); (ii) foreigners who are
well-disposed to Athens; (iii) debtors (who were disenfranchised
at Athens, hence the need for the reinstatement of their citizen
rights), and (iv) Athens' colonies. These suggestions are certainly striking and, perhaps, in the recent years of crisis following the failure of the Sicilian expedition, Athenians had grown
used to suggestions for wide-reaching reform (and a radical
oligarchic coup actually did take place just a few months after
Lysistrata was staged). But the sending of embassies aside,
could any of them have been taken seriously in contemporary
Athens?

This question becomes even more complex when we try to

clarify exactly what Lysistrata is proposing. What 'foreigners' does she mean? What does she mean by 'colonies' (scholars are unsure)? More importantly, what status do Lysistrata's words have here? Ancient theatre-goers would have been used to hearing serious-sounding pieces of 'advice' from Aristophanes in his plays, but these were normally delivered by the chorus in a direct audience address (an element missing from *Lysistrata*). So how would the various members of Aristophanes' audience have reacted to these suggestions of Lysistrata's – made ostensibly in earnest, but presented in the form of an involved metaphor by a female character in the midst of a bawdy comedy? There are no easy answers here.

Conclusion

This brief discussion of the people of *Lysistrata* has allowed us a fascinating insight into the way in which Aristophanes fashions characters for his plays – characters that are not only lively and engaging but also capable of conveying complex and radical ideas. In the case of the old men and old women of the play, everyday objects such as logs and pitchers are put to multiple uses to create a dramatically convincing and thematically rich battle of the sexes. As far as Athenian women are concerned, Aristophanes draws on comic stereotypes in an inventive way, exploiting the tension, for example, between women's supposed love of sex and the decision to hold a sex-strike to bring an end to the war. As for Spartans, he draws on popular notions of their city – such as the beauty of its women and its musical traditions – and adds in a revisionist account of inter-state relations to create what must have been a highly controversial positive portrait of its people and culture. Lastly, we have seen how women's traditional domestic activities are cleverly reconfigured by Aristophanes to create a hybrid absurd/logical model for running a state (the wool-working metaphor) which in turn contains a number of radical suggestions concerning different classes of non-citizens.

One of the most enduring questions surrounding Aristophanes' plays is the extent to which we are justified in reading a 'message' into what his characters do and say (and here we

have only the evidence of the plays to go on: we have no independent record of what Aristophanes thought or was trying to
achieve in his work). Some aspects of day-to-day existence seem
to be taken for granted in *Lysistrata* (perhaps most notably the
'housewifeyness' of women: tellingly, the play's 'happy ending'
involves women returning to the domestic sphere). Other aspects of contemporary life (Athenian attitudes towards Sparta;
the make-up of the citizen body) appear to be brought under
scrutiny – but in hugely different ways. But Aristophanes
treats none of these themes in a simple way; rather, they all
emerge in the course of a complex work of art – a play which its
writer is also concerned to make lively, amusing, dramatically
coherent, and so on. Locating any assumptions or opinions of
Aristophanes' in *Lysistrata* is no easy task, but in one sense this
makes the play all the richer. *Lysistrata* can be read and performed in different ways and take on new meanings for new
audiences. And in this way the people of *Lysistrata* – be they
friends or foes – are still talking to us across the centuries.

*

References in this essay are to line numbers in the original
Greek text. Translations are taken from the edition by A.H.
Sommerstein, *The Comedies of Aristophanes,* vol. 7: Lysistrata
(Warminster: Aris and Phillips, 1990).

6

Fantasy and Plot in *Lysistrata*

Alan Beale

In 411 BC, after twenty years of hostilities against Sparta and
her allies, and after the crushing defeat of the Sicilian expedition, Athens' prospects must have looked grim. The mood of fear
and panic when news of the Sicilian disaster reached Athens
only the previous year is graphically recorded by Thucydides
(8.1), who also reveals the resilient determination to fight on.
But how different is the world of Old Comedy! Although it deals
with contemporary issues, it creates fantasies which often seem
like wish-fulfilment dreams, where the characters, and indeed
the audience, like Alice are 'ready to accept the wildest impossi-
bilities with all that utter trust that only dreamers know' (Lewis Carroll in M. Gardner, *The Annotated Alice*, Penguin 1965).
Carroll makes the reader aware of this acceptance with the
comment 'when she thought it over afterwards, it occurred to
her that she ought to have wondered at this, but at the time it
all seemed quite natural'. Aristophanes created fantasy worlds
out of the contemporary life of Athens which function like
Wonderland in so far as things may happen in unexpected
ways, yet in the context of the play seem 'quite natural'.
   This type of fantasy had been developed by writers of Old
Comedy during the fifth century BC. Crates, for example, had
created an idlers' paradise where no one need work. To make
such a fantasy succeed, a logical plot is required, but one which
employs an internal, 'comic logic' to allow the improbable or
impossible to happen. So Aristophanes offered his audience in
411 BC a 'peace play', a vision of the end of the war with Sparta,
but with a bold idea direct from the world of fantasy: a conspir-

acy by the women of Greece to force their husbands to make peace. That is remarkable enough in a society where men have complete political control and women are largely confined to the domestic sphere. But the women are to achieve their political goal principally by domestic means: a sex-strike. The result leaves husbands with permanent and painfully distended erections. This is the essence of the comic fantasy that drives the plot. For Lysistrata's great idea, her master plan for peace, would not work without such impossibly exaggerated reaction to sexual deprivation. It is as absurd as starving the gods into submission with a wall across the sky (*Birds*) or riding to heaven on the back of a giant dung beetle (*Peace*). But the sex-strike isn't the only element of Lysistrata's scheme and the sustained erection isn't the only illogical element in the play. Aristophanes' complex plot exploits the dramatic possibilities of his fantasy's 'comic logic' in a number of surprising and ingenious ways. In the world of the play many unrealistic details are simply taken for granted. For example Aristophanes offers no explanation of how Lysistrata could have called the meeting with which the play opens, or how it could effectively assemble in an Athenian street or indeed how Spartan, Corinthian and Boeotian women could to come to Athens at all. But this essay will focus more on the dramatic presentation of the fantasy rather than such illogical details.

In the prologue (1-253) Aristophanes is intent on generating suspense to engage the audience's curiosity. He makes Lysistrata reveal her fantastic plan in stages as the other characters appear, even then revealing what she intends to achieve more readily than the way she intends to achieve it. She is first on stage, anxious that not one woman has turned up, and after her neighbour Calonice comes out (5), Lysistrata complains that the women have been told to meet to discuss something not unimportant (13-14). By line 30 it is a matter of the safety of all Greece depending on the women and finally by 50-53 it is to stop men taking up arms. When the other Athenian women do finally arrive (68), Lysistrata puts off informing them what the 'matter of importance' is until the Boeotian and Peloponnesian women appear (71-6). At line 97, Lysistrata avoids a direct answer when both Lampito and Calonice have asked what this 'serious/important' matter is. Once the women have confessed to missing their husbands, Lysistrata can ask them whether they would join her in bringing the war to an end (111-12). The final revelation (120-4) is itself interrupted and it is only with the last word in 124 that the women discover Lysistrata's proposed strategy for stopping the war: the women must abstain from sex ('cock').

The women instantly reject the idea and take some persuading that giving up sex is possible (Lysistrata has to bind them to her scheme by oath, 181ff.), a humorous response Aristophanes has carefully prepared by distinguishing Lysistrata from the others. As early as the first line he introduces stock jokes about women's unrestrained appetite for wine and sex: immediately Lysistrata appears on stage, she complains that women would have flocked to a Bacchic revel or shrine of Pan (suggested as a convenient place for sex by Cinesias in line 911). Subsequently Aristophanes generates considerable humour from Lysistrata's struggle to persuade the women to adopt her plan and to stay with it. Although she shares their feelings and aspirations – and even joins in the sexual banter (107ff.) – she is that fantasy character, the 'comic heroine', the one who has a fantastic idea and overcomes all obstacles to its success, a significant one of which is the women's sexual appetite. And yet that appetite is the wellspring of her plan, since it is not so much the safety of all Greece (29-30), the lack of Boeotian eels (702), or the bad decisions of men (as in 507-20), but their desire for their husbands to return to the marital bed that persuades the women to take action. While we hear (16-19) of the domestic chores that keep women in the house (seeing to her husband, getting the slaves working, putting baby to bed, washing and feeding it), in lines 43-5, their domestic life is quite different: wives sit tarted up with yellow dresses, cosmetics, ungirdled tunics and exotic shoes. This vision of the wife as desirable sex-object is the feed to draw her strategy from Lysistrata (46-8) and increase our curiosity and suspense: how will perfumes, make-up and slinky clothes stop men fighting? Once her plan is revealed (124), Lysistrata explains that the tantalising dress and the plucked pubic hair will inflame husbands' passions which they will then frustrate (Lampito only needs mention the disarming effect of

Helen's tits on Menelaus). Even marital rape is dismissed by Lysistrata who insists men's pleasure will be thwarted by dogged resistance and unresponsiveness.

It is frequently observed that the whole scheme is shot through with contradictions, the most obvious being that the men can't be affected by the women's action when they aren't at home, a fact we are made very much aware of in lines 99ff. where lengths of absence of five and seven months are mentioned and Lampito adds that her husband has to leave again as soon as he does get home. No acknowledgement is given to the availability of sex with slave girls, catamites or prostitutes. No provision is made for the unmarried girls (they are simply ignored, with one notable exception). Masturbation isn't mentioned. But in the fantasy world of the play such contradictions and omissions (if they are noticed at all) are more amusing for their boldness than worrying for their illogicality. But Aristophanes has revealed only the first part of this 'comic logic'. The cause may promise effect, but did the audience know just what effect to expect? Aristophanes gives nothing away just yet.

For most of the prologue Lysistrata's plan for the wives to withhold their sexual favours is all that is revealed. But then there is a surprise. At line 170 Lampito questions the women's ability to control the Athenian rabble – and especially access to the boundless funds in Athena's care on the Acropolis. Lysistrata replies that the oldest women have been *given orders* to *seize* the Acropolis. The military language suggests Lysistrata has marshalled the old women into a sort of army of occupation, an idea almost as absurd as the sex-strike. Up to this point there was only the domestic plot and only wives involved. Now women have invaded the public sphere and the audience's amusement at the notion must have been enhanced by its sudden introduction. This secondary action appears 'quite natural' to those on stage: Lampito doesn't question its feasibility but is instantly satisfied. At line 240 a shout indicates that the old women have already seized the Acropolis.

Aristophanes handles the location of the action with superb comic licence. The opening scene is set in an Athenian street (5), but when Lampito departs, the Athenian women do not return to their houses. Instead Lysistrata leads them onto the

Acropolis. The shift of scene is unobtrusively managed: Lysistrata simply announces that they will go in to join 'the other women' (245) on the Acropolis, and by 'these gates' (250-1) she indicates that the central door in the *skene* now represents the Propylaea, the monumental entrance to the Acropolis. The domestic scene is temporarily forgotten as Lysistrata and Calonice talk not of seductive dresses and perfume but of barring doors, threats and fire, although Calonice still swears by Aphrodite while claiming women are invincible in battle. Aristophanes now proceeds to make clever use of this new location. Firstly, as the Acropolis, it will be the scene for the chorus of old men's feeble assault on the women and the confrontation of Lysistrata and the Proboulos (254-705). Then for the famous scene of Cinesias' sexual assault, it will become (in line 911) Pan's grotto, just below the Acropolis, a place sacred to a suitably lustful deity. But that real setting yields to fantasy as the props used by Myrrhine for her seductive teasing (a bed, a mattress, a pillow, a blanket and perfume of two varieties) are those of the household and recall the scenario of domestic seduction imagined by Lysistrata (149ff.). The boundaries between the domestic and public spaces have been dissolved in fantasy Athens.

The occupation of the Acropolis dominates the stage for a substantial part of the play (254-705). It is introduced before the audience can see the arousal/refusal tactic in operation, allowing Aristophanes to keep the audience in suspense: the mention of the women's powerful erotic effect on their husbands (551-4) offers a strong hint of eventual success, and references to the women taking action to save Greece (524-5) and to Lampito and the Theban Ismene (696-7) are more subtle reminders. It also allows scope for different types of humour. It begins with a semi-chorus of old men coming (unfeasibly quickly) to take back the Acropolis. But it is a Grandad's Army: they struggle with their load of wood, complaining of sore shoulders, and the fire they have brought stings their eyes with smoke as they try to keep it alight. In fantasy Athens, the home guard is magnificently pathetic and spectacularly old: they recall their part in the siege of the Spartan king Cleomenes on the Acropolis almost a hundred years previously in 508 BC (273-80). The comic treatment of this episode is typical of the way that Aristophanes puts a spin on historical events to give his Athenian audience an opportunity to laugh at their enemies and feel good about themselves. Herodotus (5.72) merely reports that 'on the third day all the Spartans left under truce', but Aristophanes embellishes the story with details of the Spartans ignominiously retreating, dirty, poorly clad and having surrendered their arms. To say the Spartans were unwashed for six years is a subjection of Spartan bathing habits to extreme hyperbole. These are fantasy Spartans.

With the arrival of the semi-chorus of old women a battle of the sexes begins. Old men fighting old women for the citadel of Athens itself is as absurd as the sex-strike and brilliantly plotted to offer 'something completely different'. The women have brought water-jars. In the ensuing altercation they produce the more imaginative threats and then drench the men. Their liquid dousing of the fires which prevents the use of logs to force an entry into the shrine of the virgin goddess Athena gives this scene a thematic connection with the sex-strike, as do the references to women's wantonness (especially in the use of *double entendre*) and the exchange over crow-bars when the Proboulos arrives. The Proboulos reveals the effectiveness of Lysistrata's plan, since he has come for money to pay for oars but is thwarted by the women's occupation. The scene with the Proboulos and Lysistrata continues the armed struggle for the possession of the Acropolis. Here the old women first terrify the Scythian archers with threats, then a corps of market hags routs them in proper military fashion while Lysistrata gives the orders. This unrealistic combat and unlikely victory is attributed to two sorts of women given the terrifyingly comic names 'seed-market-pease-pudding-vegetable-sellers' and 'garlic-land-lady-bread-sellers'. The reality of the marketplace has now entered the fantasy world.

The scene with the Proboulos completes the political overthrow of male authority (507-38). His failure to acknowledge that the women are in control and his insistence on their subservience lead to a comic reversal as he is unceremoniously dragged into the fantasy world and into a woman's role: Lysistrata's veil is put round his head, he is given a basket and told to start carding wool. 'Let war be women's business'(538), Lysistrata declares, revamping the words the Proboulos had approved of, that 'war should be man's business' (520). These words of Hector to Andromache are quoted from the famous scene in the *Iliad* (6, 492). Even the world of Homer is turned upside down! Lysistrata also offers the Proboulos advice on the conduct of affairs in terms of the quintessential domestic and female activity of woolworking (574ff.). The metaphor is absolutely appropriate. Woolworking is about bringing together disparate elements into a unified whole – a cloak for the people as she puts it, a comforting image with which Aristophanes dresses up his fantasy of political domesticity. And he uses it again in the final peace negotiations. Lysistrata, in reminding the Athenians of the Spartan role in liberating Athens from the tyranny of Hippias (Spartan intervention now getting approval), says the Spartans replaced the rough slaves' costumes of the Athenians with a cloak for the people (1155). Lysistrata's treatment of the Proboulos gives a sharper focus to the fantasy of women triumphing in the men's domain. The occupation plot began with the anxiety Lampito expressed about Athenian warships and the money to build and equip them (173-4), but this is reduced to the absurd idea of the women building ships to sail against the men (674-5), which is also a reprise of a joke (sailing = having sex) used in line 60, and in both cases it is women on top.

Aristophanes returns to the sex-strike indirectly (706ff.). For it proves to be the women who are unable to maintain their abstinence from sex and several attempt to escape from the Acropolis to return to their homes. No sitting at home in seductive clothes to provoke their husbands' desire, these women are instead virtual prisoners on the Acropolis, their imaginative escape methods thwarted by Lysistrata who finally convinces them by suddenly producing an oracle (767ff.). This scene serves as a clever transition from the occupation of the Acropolis back to the sex-strike, prolonging suspense about the effect on the men and allowing more fun at the expense of the women.

In the scene beginning at line 830 we at long last see that the sex-strike is having the desired effect. Aristophanes has kept us in suspense, but now is ready to spring his big comic surprise. Cinesias, whose name and deme constitute puns equivalent to

Roger of Ramsgate, is seen by the women. He is arriving in a state of arousal, as we finally see on his entry in line 845, the first revelation that husbands, both Athenian and Spartan, are afflicted with permanent and painfully distended erections. Now, encouraged by Lysistrata, Myrrhine puts the seduction tactic into action. Her provocation/prevarication keeps both audience and Cinesias on toast and provides most of the humour in this famous scene. One of the props in this scene is put to subtle use by Aristophanes: the baby, which Cinesias has brought with him. First, like the Proboulos' wool, it maintains the fantasy of role reversal, making the domestic sphere the place of the man while the woman is away on martial rather than marital duties, a reversal of the basic reason for the strike. Secondly, the baby (or the baby's neglect) is used by Cinesias to lure Myrrhine down from the ramparts. In doing this Cinesias reveals that this is the sixth day the baby has gone without a wash or breastfeeding. This joke at the expense of the man's incompetent child-rearing, like the main plot, ignores the options available in the real world (the female slaves, a wet nurse) but amuses by its hyperbole – the thought of an infant unwashed and unsuckled for so long isn't pretty. It also serves to mark the passage of time to allow the male arousal to become desperate – for which it is, of course, comically inadequate, even though the likely speed of male capitulation was remarked on by Lysistrata in line 154. The baby is also employed for what has been termed a 'boomerang joke': Cinesias' use of the child as an enticement recoils on him as he is trumped by Myrrhine for whom it becomes the first of her delaying tactics – how could they do it in front of the child? Once removed, the child would seem to have performed its role, but in the unreal world of Aristophanes there is a strange verbal metamorphosis. At the end of the scene Myrrhine leaves Cinesias at the peak of arousal and frustration. 'Who shall I fuck?' he asks, but then, 'How shall I see to this child?' He refers of course to his erect phallus and caps the joke by asking where a pimp is, then ordering a wet nurse!

The sex-strike has worked, but Cinesias' capitulation isn't complete until, in the scene with the Spartan Herald who has arrived in a similar distended condition, it finally dawns on him

(1008) that it is an international conspiracy. At that point he sends the Herald off to Sparta to arrange for delegates to be sent to conclude a peace settlement while he himself will ask the Council in Athens. With men routed by women in battle, politics reduced to woolworking, husbands afflicted with permanent priapism, Aristophanes' conclusion of his fantasy peace had to be good. And he rises to the occasion. He raises expectation of reconciliation which was demanded by Myrrhine (900 and 932), sought by the Spartan Herald (984) and has become a shared goal by line 1009.

And then, when Reconciliation is called out onto the stage, her arrival (1114) is a *coup de théâtre*: she is no abstract noun, but a naked woman, Reconciliation, the embodiment of all that the men might wish for. She is sexual pleasure, fecundity and desirable territory to be partitioned so that both Athenians and Spartans receive (sexually) gratifying terms despite their initial reluctance. Thus enticed, both cannot wait to get down to farming (Sommerstein's 'husbandry' captures the wordplay). Peace is concluded with the usual feasting and drinking (the Spartans turn out to be agreeable company) until Lysistrata restores the wives to their husbands. Couples are reunited and the play ends as they dance (presumably) together.

A finale with Spartans dancing and praising Sparta? In Aristophanes' fantasy world this might be 'quite natural' and in the festive occasion of the performance it might be hugely entertaining, but even within the fantasy the reality of war was not forgotten. In lines 590ff. Lysistrata gives a reminder of the harsh sacrifices that women must make in war. They bear sons and send out those children as soldiers, but before she can add 'to die' the Proboulos silences her. Furthermore, the absence of men deprives the women of their pleasure, but this relatively innocuous recollection of the plot's essential motivation is followed by a glimpse of a grimmer reality: virgin spinsters growing old, indeed too old for marriage at all. In 411 BC this must have been a harsh intrusion into the fantasy of the play. The Proboulos' response is cut short before he can show any further insensitivity on the subject.

7

On Misunderstanding the *Lysistrata*, Productively

Martin Revermann

(*The women, in a circle, place their right hands together.*)

Lampito	Keep it zipped till they flip!
Women	Keep it zipped till they flip!
Dipsas	Cross your legs or hope to die!
Women	Cross your legs or hope to die!
Myrrhine	Don't give them a piece of ass, until they give us a peace that lasts!
Women	Don't give them a piece of ass, until they give us a peace that lasts!
Calonice	Make love, not war!
Women	Make love, not war!

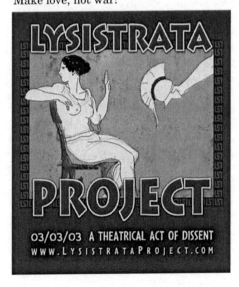

7. On Misunderstanding the Lysistrata, Productively

Ellen McLaughlin's adaptation of Aristophanes' *Lysistrata*, from which this brief sequence is taken, was part of a bigger scheme. The 'Lysistrata Project: A Theatrical Act of Dissent' [*see opposite*] figured as a means of global protest against the looming Iraq War. On 3 March 2003, days before the first bombs were dropped on Baghdad, the play was performed in 59 countries, usually as a reading, in front of an audience estimated to have exceeded 300,000 (see Lorna Hardwick in this volume). McLaughlin's script, in her own words 'a short and sweet version' (it lasted for about an hour), was put on as a reading in New York at the Brooklyn Academy of Music. The phallic theme, indispensable for the play's comic effect and a main feature of its visual dimension, was introduced into the reading by means of a female clown who, before the performance, would sit in the audience pumping up large balloons of unmistakeable shape.

It was, of course, more than just 'a bunch of Ancient Greek dick jokes with some acrobatics thrown in to fill out the evening', as McLaughlin makes Cinesias say. Rarely, in fact, in its colourful reception history has the play been more blatantly politicised than on that Monday in 2003. McLaughlin's use of the motto 'Make love, not war!', deeply reminiscent to an Anglophone audience not just of the anti-Vietnam movement but of the hippie culture and sexual liberation movement of the 1960s in general, is an honest and revealing shorthand of what the play stands for to audiences world-wide in the late twentieth and early twenty-first centuries: a proto-feminist play that advocates pacifism. In the pages which follow, I will discuss both these features against the context of the play's performance in Athens in 411 BC. As will emerge, both the proto-feminist and the pacifist readings of the play are demonstrably wrong. But this is not where classicists can, or should, stop. When contemporary audiences are reading something into the play which is either not there (feminism) or not quite there (pacifism), they evidently do so for a reason: they are projecting something onto the ancient play which helps, or perhaps enables them in the first place, to interact with it in ways that are meaningful to them. This kind of productive misreading, as I would like to call it, is neither a threat to historical purism nor a fashionable aberration of taste. It would seem that it is a necessary part of making the ancient text 'ours', and as such commands the attention, and respect, of all of us who are, in various ways, professionally interested in ancient culture.

A proto-feminist play?

If *Lysistrata* had been conceived, and perceived, as a feminist play in its fifth-century BC context, this would be highly exceptional. Much thought and time has been invested over the past forty years into improving our understanding of gender and gender relations not just in ancient Greece but in Western (and global) culture in general. As a result, the notion of women in antiquity as perpetually locked-up and entirely suppressed has been replaced with a considerably more nuanced one. In ancient Greece of all periods women played a vital part in religious life, occupying important priesthoods, celebrating key festivals (with or without men) and performing in specialised functions as worshippers of the gods (maiden choruses in honour of various deities, for instance, are well-attested for all of Greece – except Athens, curiously enough). Some women were highly educated (including some who belonged to the sub-elite, especially courtesans), and female artists could be well-known celebrities (like the poets Sappho and Corinna). In aristocratic households, they would often command considerable actual power, while they were indispensable bread-winners in smaller urban families or in the agriculture-based rural environment.

Yet it also remains true that women, throughout antiquity, were not treated as full human beings. They had no political voice, and were debarred from any official means of political participation. Like slaves, they were not legal subjects and could not own land. Against this reality, the representation of Lysistrata (and other women in both comedy and tragedy) stands out even more, because she is, precisely, so eminently *political*. Is Aristophanes the enlightened, progressive thinker who anticipates emancipation and the women's rights movement by more than two millennia? Surely not. One crucial thing to realise is that putting a woman into a position of political authority, control and power in a comedy is an important part

of the humour. It is *funny*, straightforwardly ridiculous, because it blatantly (and fantastically) defies the reality of the
world of the audience.

This fundamental point applies regardless of whether or not
there were women present in the fifth-century BC Athenian
audience. The question is disputed and, on the evidence currently available, cannot be answered conclusively. All
addresses by actors to the audience – and there are quite a few
(even though they all occur in comedy and none in tragedy or
satyr play) – are to men. But this need not mean that there
were only men present. It may well be the case that only men
are addressed because only men were thought to matter (they
would, then, constitute the so-called notional audience which in
this case would not be identical with the actual audience). In
fact I believe that there is evidence to suggest that women *were*
present in the fifth-century BC Athenian theatre (it comes not
from drama but from Plato's *Gorgias* (502d2-8), a dialogue
probably composed in the first quarter of the fourth century BC).
If women were indeed present, it is fascinating to speculate how
they would have responded to seeing a Lysistrata or Medea on
stage. Would they have felt empowered, or estranged and alien-
ated (as most men probably were)? One thing they certainly did
not do: get organised to advocate social change and gender
equality.

Funny and entertaining as the presence of fantastically empowered women on the comic stage may be in itself, there are
other clear indications that there is no agenda whatsoever of
proto-feminism in Aristophanes' play. One surely must be the
fact that Lysistrata's empowerment is only temporary, and
indeed aimed from the start at giving power *back* to the men
once they have been brought to their senses and stopped the
war. 'However, the conflict over, the danger passed, the new
roles are generally relinquished even if the experience is there
to draw on. The woman warrior, metaphorically speaking, shed
her armour and put flowers in her hair.' This quote from the
book *The Prospect Before Her* (p. 489) by Olwen Hufton, a
leading historian of gender relations in the early modern period
and taken from a very different context, is quite applicable to
what is going on in *Lysistrata*. Once the Athenians and Spar-

tans have been reconciled through Lysistrata's forceful media-
tion, the status quo is restored, politically, socially and
sexually. Lysistrata and her fellow-conspirators have served
their purpose, and willingly acquiesce with the way things used
to be.

In addition, the representation of women in comedy is not all
that complimentary, another indicator that gender equality
and female empowerment were not at all on Aristophanes'
agenda (or on that of his audience). Aristophanic women are not
models of virtue and chastity. They are scheming, vulgar and
show a notable lack of self-control, a common misogynist charge
in ancient Greece which expresses itself in an insatiable appetite for alcohol and sex (it forms the basis for the humour of the
opening scene in *Lysistrata*).

This picture is, however, complicated by the fact that there is
one single female figure in preserved comedy who is curiously
exempt from most of these stock characteristics: Lysistrata!
Although the play constantly activates genre-typical stereotypes, the protagonist herself is exceptionally intelligent and
self-controlled, with little to suggest that she shares the faults
which her fellow-conspirators show so abundantly (and enter-
tainingly). This may make her a bit of a boring comic heroine:
sober, entirely rational, non- or even asexual (a husband, who is
of no overall relevance, is, however, mentioned at 513-20). The
notion of a comic heroine who is in total control (not least of
herself) and towers above that 'all-too-humanness' of women in
comedy certainly facilitates bringing the big comic project to
fruition and integrating the two sub-plots (sex-strike and occupation of the acropolis) into one.

In addition, some (myself included: see also in this volume
Edith Hall, pp. 32f., James Robson, p. 52 and Alan Sommerstein, p. 46) have taken very seriously the possibility that the
figure of Lysistrata is somewhat modelled on that of the priestess of Athena Polias ('protectress of the city'), Lysimache by
name, who was holding office when the play was performed in
Athens in 411 BC (at which festival is not entirely clear, probably the Lenaea which took place in January/February).
Particularly in the final sequence of the play Lysistrata undoubtedly acquires a special, almost Athena-like status as the

grand mediator on the Acropolis (which is where the play is set, a very unusual choice in both comedy and tragedy). If the priestess Lysimache (whose name means 'dissolver of battle', something very similar to Lysistrata, 'dissolver of the army') indeed provided some kind of a model for Lysistrata, the above-mentioned peculiarities of this character would start to make even more sense. But whoever and whatever Lysistrata 'is', it is clear who and what she is not: a women's rights advocate.

A pacifist play?

As with proto-feminism, pacifism too would be highly exceptional if present. Fundamental opposition to war as a means of conflict resolution is not attested for antiquity at all. No known philosophical school, for instance, opposes war, even if some of them challenge other fundamentals of the human experience like the existence of the gods or the value of communal and political life. On the contrary, some philosophers appear to have given conflict a prominently productive role in their philosophies. Thus Heraclitus (c. 540-c. 480 BC) famously proclaimed that 'war (*polemos*) is the father of all things' (though what precisely is meant by this is not easy to see, not surprisingly with a philosopher who in antiquity bore the nickname 'the obscure one'). For Empedocles (born in the early fifth century) 'love' (*philia*) and 'strife' (*neikos*) are the forces that make up the cosmos. Hesiod, famously, distinguishes between good and bad 'conflict' (*eris*) (*Works and Days* 11-26). That there is no aversion to conflict does not come as a surprise in a society as competitive as the ancient Greek one. This is often called the 'agonal' nature (*agon* = competition) of ancient Greek society, a feature first recognised in modern times as being of central importance by the Swiss cultural historian Jacob Burckhardt (1818-97).

That said, war (defined as military conflict) is rarely glorified. The (sparsely) preserved poetry by the Spartan poet Tyrtaeus (seventh century) comes to mind. In his verses there can be no question about the elevation of fighting and death in battle (that this kind of poetry was, among other contexts, performed to – or by – soldiers as or shortly before they would enter battle is a very plausible hypothesis). But a much more nuanced view of war clearly prevails.

In the *Iliad*, the foundational poem of Greek culture, war is a necessity, but an awful, disgusting and terrible one. The standard expression used is 'levelling war' (*omoiios polemos*): war leaves no winners and unites human beings in the ultimate realisation of their own mortality. In the final book of the *Iliad*, Priam, having ransomed from Achilles the body of his son Hector, sets out that during the agreed truce the Trojans will lament Hector for nine days, bury him and build a mound on days ten and eleven, 'but on the twelfth day we will fight, if it is indeed necessary (*ei per ananke*)' (*Iliad* 24.667). Given that the *Iliad* is a poem about war, it is remarkable that the poem is far from glorifying it (even if war remains an outstanding opportunity for humans to distinguish themselves).

Lysistrata, as mentioned earlier, means 'dissolver of the army', and the express purpose of her grand scheme is to make Spartans and Athenians stop fighting each other. But it is this particular conflict that she has in mind, not war itself. The distinction is explicitly made in her big speech of reconciliation towards the end of the play (1133f.): '... while enemies are at hand with their barbarian armies you destroy Greek men and cities'. It is war among Greeks, and not war itself, which she and her fellow-conspirators want to put an end to. 'Make love not the *Peloponnesian* War' is her message to the fifth-century audience. Is a twenty-first-century audience willing, and able, to listen to *that*?

On misunderstanding, or: are the contemporary readings of the play wrong?

There is a short answer to this one: yes. Against the backdrop of historical contextualisation, both the proto-feminist and the pacifist readings are wrong and easily falsifiable. But there is another, and much more fascinating, answer. It involves asking why exactly the play is almost invariably misread. Is it ignorance or negligent reading? This might sometimes be the case, especially since in common perception the ancient Greeks are often thought to have been the first to have come up with something very important. The Athenians, for instance, are regularly presented as proto-democratic, as the inventors of democracy, even though it is deeply problematic to apply this term to a society which, while widening the scope of political participation and eligibility for public office, continued to deny these and many other rights to women and slaves (quite apart from the historical fact that Athens was not the first democratic system on Greek soil to begin with).

But there is, to be sure, something deeper going on. Lysistrata *is*, after all, a very powerful woman, and war *is* considered to be an evil (even if a necessary one). For a modern mind, it seems, the step towards projecting feminism and pacifism into the play is not only an extremely small but even a necessary one. The play *has* to be read along those lines – for only then does it matter to us. Contemporary recipients are profoundly conditioned, or one might even say 'hardwired', to view the play through such perceptual filters. In the wake of two World Wars and a chilling Cold War, and with the continued possibility of nuclear annihilation hovering above our heads, audiences in the late twentieth and early twenty-first century cannot but see Lysistrata's resistance to war among Greeks as opposition to war itself. And her distinct, courageous and charismatic voice is bound to be heard as that of an emancipated woman. This is nothing which competent and historically aware classicists could, or should, fight. After all, the play's modern reception forces classicists to ask very interesting questions about their own field of inquiry (what, for example, do we as classicists make of the fact that the female voice in Greek drama is so prominent and complex when it is being silenced in almost all other public discourses?). More importantly, however, classicists should be extremely pleased to see that a play created so long ago continues to speak to everyone in the present world – even if we cannot help listening to it in our own ways.

Further reading

The best translation of *Lysistrata* is the one by Stephen Halliwell (Oxford: Oxford University Press, 1997). It is available in paperback in the Oxford World's Classics series (together with *Birds, Assembly-Women* and *Wealth*). The volume also has very useful notes and features an excellent introduction. It is on a par, and should be used in conjunction with, Kenneth Dover's un-superseded monograph *Aristophanic Comedy* (Berkeley: University of California Press, 1972).

The play in its performative context is discussed by Martin Revermann in *Comic Business: Theatricality, Dramatic Technique and Performance Contexts of Aristophanic Comedy* (Oxford: Oxford University Press, 2006), 236-60. McLaughlin's version for the 'Lysistrata Project' in 2003 is available in Ellen McLaughlin, *The Greek Plays* (New York: Theatre Communications Group, Inc., 2006).

On women in antiquity see the fine and richly illustrated volume by Elaine Fantham and Helene Foley (eds), *Women in the Classical World* (Oxford: Oxford University Press, 1995). On women in Aristophanes there is Lauren Taaffe's *Aristophanes and Women* (London and New York: Routledge, 1993) and Helene Foley's piece on gender in *The Cambridge Companion to Greek Comedy* (edited by Martin Revermann, forthcoming 2011). For how historical gender studies can be done, it is worth having a look at Olwen Hufton's magisterial *The Prospect Before Her: A History of Women in Western Europe,* vol. 1: *1500-1800* (London: HarperCollins, 1995).

As regards the study of modern reception of Greek drama a superb study is Edith Hall's introduction to Edith Hall, Fiona Macintosh and Amanda Wrigley (eds), *Dionysus Since 69: Greek Tragedy at the Dawn of the Third Millennium* (Oxford: Oxford University Press, 2004), 1-46 (focusing on tragedy). The whole volume, a collection of more than a dozen of articles, is of very high quality. Cultural drivers for why and how we continue to connect to Greek drama are identified in Martin Revermann's article 'The Appeal of Dystopia: Latching onto Greek Drama in the 20th Century' (*Arion* 16, 2008, 97-117).

For locating information about individual performances the online-database of the *Archive of Performances of Greek and Roman Drama* (http://www.apgrd.ox.ac.uk) is indispensable. On the Lysistrata Project, see M. Kotzamani's article, 'Artist

Citizens in the Age of the Web: The Lysistrata Project (2003-Present)' (*Theater* 36, 2006, 103-10).

On the modern reception of Aristophanes in general, see Gonda van Steen's contribution to *The Cambridge Companion to Greek Comedy* (edited by Martin Revermann, forthcoming 2011).

8

*Lysistrata*s on the Modern Stage

Lorna Hardwick

The performance history of *Lysistrata* in the last hundred years offers us a map of shifting attitudes to the relationships between politics and gender and between these and the aesthetics of theatre. In that respect, whatever the particular settings, the translations, versions and adaptations engage directly with Aristophanes' relationship to the theatrical, social and political environment of his own times. In the West, the play has been by far the most frequently performed Aristophanic comedy.

In the early twentieth century, productions and adaptations of *Lysistrata* were important in addressing women's struggle to obtain a social and political voice and in challenging the prurience that had marginalised the play. The play also provided a stimulus to aesthetic experiments in theatrical modernism, for example in Max Reinhardt's Berlin production of 1908 and the 1923 version directed for the Moscow Art Theatre's Musical Studio by Nemirovich-Danchenko inspired by the October Revolution of 1917 (Kotzamani 2005). These early twentieth-century productions established associations between the play's focus on city life and politics and the contemporary idealisation of novelty and politically engaged theatre. They exploited the association between the setting in the city of Athens, the Acropolis and the (sometimes fuzzy) construction of links with modern democratic values.

There are, however, some more socially conservative aspects present in an earlier example of a 'revolutionary' production of the play. François-Benoît Hoffmann's *Lisitrata* aroused the wrath of the censors in 1801-2. Staged in France during the negotiations for the peace treaty of Amiens, the play was described as 'a Comedy in one act and in prose, mixed with satirical songs and imitating Aristophanes' play: its performances have been suspended by Order' (Orfanos 2007, 106). Interestingly, in this particular adaptation the women were pretty feeble. They abandoned their sex-strike and gave up the peace-making initiative to men. The author re-domesticated the women and probably fell foul of Napoleon's censors because of the play's irreverent treatment of war. The incident demonstrates the sometimes uneasy balance between viewing the play as a comment on war and as a comment on women's voices in the political process. It also raises questions about the extent to which the two are thought either to work together or at least to be compatible.

The key aspects of modern responses to Aristophanes are at the intersections between the logical and the fantastic (see James Robson and Alan Beale in this volume) and between gender and the political. This raises issues about how social groups are represented and in particular about the degree of reconciliation between theatrical exploitation of the comic potential of stereotypes and a more naturalistic representation of the possibilities and limits of social action. In Aristophanes, the ways in which the women's actions are represented point up their incongruity in the 'real' environment at Athens and play with the relationship between gender assumptions and the authority of political judgements and actions. Aristophanes was able to explore contentious issues concerning the Peloponnesian War of 431-404 BC by situating these in alignment with a conception of women's self-empowerment that was, and would be seen to be, impossible. In contrast, in the twentieth- and the early twenty-first centuries, the cultural contexts of Western Europe and the United States have gradually conceded some kind of political role to women, ranging from the franchise to active participation as politicians and opinion-makers (although at the time of writing in spring 2008 the sexist and misogynistic language used by mainstream media and commentators on both sides of the Atlantic to attack and trivialise Senator Hillary Clinton's bid to become the Democratic candidate in the US Presidential election should caution against complacency in this respect).

Contemporary productions have sometimes elided gender and anti-war themes, as in Tony Harrison's *The Common Chorus* (1988/1992), in which the play was set in the context of the Greenham Common Women's Peace Camp protests against the stationing of US missiles in the UK. However, the most prominent recent exploration of the play's potential for consciousness-raising has been in the Lysistrata Project of 2003. This was a world-wide initiative organised to protest against the imminent invasion of Iraq by the United States-led coalition, which included the UK and Australia. The Project involved over a thousand co-ordinated readings from *Lysistrata*, held all over the world on 3 March 2003.

The project was initiated and organised by two New York-based actors, Kathryn Blume and Sharron Bower. At a cost of $35 dollars to set up the server space they used the internet to spread information. The letter posted on their website invited people to take on responsibility for trying to avert war by participating in 'a theatrical act of dissent'. The wording of the letter appealed directly to people's emotions and sense of political impotence:

> Are you frustrated by the build up to war? Do you fell as if there isn't something you can do? Well. Here's something you CAN do. Do a reading of *Lysistrata* on March 3 and be part of the Lysistrata Project.

The initiative mobilised over 300,000 people who participated in readings in fifty-nine countries (which was documented by its own website). The whole operation took a little over six weeks to set up. It brought together the communication and mobilisation capacity of the internet and the reputation of *Lysistrata* as a play that was not only one of protest and transgression but also one in which activists could express their views and seek to bring about change (in that respect they did not succeed in averting the war; they did mobilise opinion).

There was a wide variety of readings and creative responses. These ranged from epic drama to documentary theatre to multimedia versions to storytelling. In London, actors read a version in front of the Houses of Parliament. They wore blindfolds which they tore off and waved, becoming what they called 'a chorus of disapproval'. In New York, at Grand Central Station, a storyteller performed a children's version which began with the words: 'In the very old days in ancient Greece, women didn't used to do the same jobs as men did. Women swept and dusted and tidied their houses ... but men knew nothing else but making war.' These examples are included in the account written by the academic and dramaturge Marina Kotzamani for the *Performing Arts Journal* (*PAJ*). She also records that in Holland (Hilversum) a radio documentary combined excerpts from Aristophanes with interviews with politicians and reports from war zones, while in Israel storytellers were organised to go out into communities and tell the story of Lysistrata in as many places as possible.

In Greece itself there was an interesting contrast between two readings that took place in Athens and in Patras. The Athens reading took place on the Pnyx, on the south-eastern slope of the Acropolis and the site of the ancient Athenian *ekklesia* (assembly). The reading aimed to celebrate democracy and to involve the city in general – passers-by and tourists as well as those who watched televised excerpts. There was a carnival atmosphere with participants costumed in long wigs, huge breasts and *phalloi* that replicated the ancient performance tradition. The reading also proclaimed the confidence of modern women in occupying and using a public space that in ancient Athens was the territory of men.

The Patras reading was very different in participants and in tone. It used the neoclassical ruins of an old marketplace in the centre of the city. This site was being used as a social centre by Kurdish political refugees, and the *Lysistrata* reading (which was organised by Panos Kouros, an academic at the School of Architecture in the city) involved about fifty people, including male refugees and architecture students. Part of the event took place in candlelight after a power cut. Kouros recounted how 'we could see our shadows in the white tent and we could feel more the voices. This created a very strong feeling of humanity, and a sense of sharing the same hopes and fears. We spoke in ancient Greek (text), modern Greek (text and dialogues), some English and Kurdish (through spontaneous translations). We also talked a lot with our eyes, our movement and our body. We drank tea' (quoted in Kotzamani, *Theater* 36.2, p. 105). As a protest against the war in Iraq this was an ambivalent reading because the Kurds were refugees from Saddam Hussein's regime and hoped that his overthrow would enable them to return. Yet they also (presciently as it turned out) recognised the war as involving US expansion and aggression.

Most of the readings in the Lysistrata Project took place in the West. However, some Arabic countries bordering the Mediterranean also took part, and Marina Kotzamani subsequently used this as a springboard for an imaginative exploration of the play's potential as a catalyst in non-Western cultures. In 2004 she organised a project in which she invited Arab theatre practitioners, playwrights and theorists to outline in writing how they would stage *Lysistrata* in their own countries. She presented and discussed the results at a conference in Morocco in 2005 and published an article in *PAJ* (from which the quotations subsequently used in this discussion are taken).

Most of the respondents were male and were well-established theatre professionals. Responses seemed to follow the trend set by the 2003 Lysistrata Project in that they framed the play in a global context and examined critically the relationship between autocracy, imperialism and manipulation of the media. Most responses doubted that the war between Athenians and Spartans portrayed in Aristophanes' play provided an adequate basis for probing the complexities of war in today's world. Several contributors pointed out that the Peloponnesian War was fought between states who shared a common framework of ethnicity, religious practices, culture and values. It was, as Hazem Azmy put it, 'an internecine war'.

Some of the reasons given for not accepting the Aristophanic situation as a viable model for contemporary theatre are revealing of both ancient and modern approaches. For instance, Khaled El Sawy, the Egyptian playwright and director, saw problems about who could be seen to take a peace initiative. If the Athenian women were identified with Arab women this could be interpreted as having the weaker party sue for peace ('To preach a message of peace to today's Arab audiences is tantamount to instructing the victims to accept sheepishly the dictates of their arrogant oppressors'). He therefore cast the women seeking peace as American rather than Arab and set the play in the US using a performance idiom based on the rock operas of the 1970s. His approach mixed the light-hearted conventions of the musical with tragic-comedy, parody and the grotesque in order to create a powerful political theatre. He used the Aristophanic concept of the double Chorus to express the alternative voices of the city. A sexy Chorus of Hollywood blondes co-existed with a more restrained chorus that included African-Americans and provided links to a diverse audience. However, the outcome to his visualisation of the play was deeply pessimistic – the conclusion of peace was immediately followed by sirens and explosions signalling the continuation of war and the limits of popular activism in contemporary situations. The Palestinian director George Ibrahim took these doubts further, saying that he could not use *Lysistrata* to address the conflict between Israelis and Palestinians because he considered there were crucial differences between the ancient and modern situations (such as Israeli army occupation of Palestinian territory and guerrilla resistance).

Most of the responders saw Aristophanes' play as a people's play rather than as an exploration of the possibilities of women's action. However, two of the respondents did express interest in linking gender to the opposition between war and peace. They produced synopses that were critical of patriarchal systems and aggressive masculinity and that associated women with a more genuine desire for peace. Ghada Amer (a visual artist originally from Cairo and now based in New York) wished to examine the role of the female chorus on a number of levels. She wanted this chorus to be played by men in order to demonstrate that women in a patriarchal society do not have self-possession. She imagined the (male) actors in the female chorus as wearing hoods to present the domination of men over women as that of minds over bodies. The image also had more literal links with the abuse of Iraqi prisoners by US guards at the Abu Ghraib prison. This is a useful reminder of the way in which costume and somatic language can create resonances that cross cultures as well as time-spans.

One of the respondents, the celebrated Egyptian film director and playwright Lenin El-Ramly, used the initiative as inspiration for writing a full-length play based on *Lysistrata*. His play, *Salam El-Nisaa* (*A Peace of Women*) was produced in Cairo in December 2004 and led to considerable discussion in the Egyptian press. It is now being translated in English by Hazem Azmy under the editorial supervision of Professor Marvin Carlson at CUNY (extracts available at http://www.wordswithoutborders.org). El-Ramly described his motivation as 'initially for no other purpose except to see how the censor would react to it' (El-Ramly 2005a, 175). This response is linked, perhaps, to his view that it was not coincidence 'that the art of theatre should be born in the lap of Athenian democracy ... the essence of all drama is inner conflict, democracy being the recognition of this conflict within the one society'. He also comments on how frequently that kind of conflict is 'conveniently and manipulatively [turned] into an external one with a national dimension' (El-Ramly 2005b). His comment provides a timely warning about the complexities involved in assessing any appropriation of Greek drama.

El-Ramly's play was set in Baghdad shortly before the US-led invasion, and the Chorus of Old Men in Aristophanes was replaced with a Chorus of Iraqi anti-riot police. The Iraqi Lysistrata allied herself with American and other Western women activists and occupied the Ministry of Petroleum. However, in contrast to the Aristophanes, the Iraqi and American officials made an alliance against the transgressive women, who in turn became progressively more divided by their different cultural and moral value systems. In his discussion of the play (El-Ramly 2005a, 2005b), El-Ramly also points out that he had to develop techniques for communicating Aristophanes' use of sexual puns and jokes. Previous translations of the play into Arabic had bowdlerised some of these passages. El-Ramly found that by using *Fus'ha* (Modern Standard Arabic) for the first time in his career he could get round some of these problems since, he says, *Fus'ha* has an abstract quality that allows it to suggest meaning with explicit statement. This is in contrast to the everyday *Ammega* (Egyptian Colloquial Arabic) into which the audience would mentally 'translate' the play-text. Thus he created a kind of internal cultural movement in the spectators' minds.

El-Ramly had a further problem in staging his play, since his concept did not fit the requirements of either the commercial or the state-run theatres. He obtained funding from the Greek community in Egypt and directed the play himself with an amateur cast. It was staged in the open-air theatre of the Opera House. He commented wryly, 'As I knew at the time, few Egyptian amateur actresses were indeed ready to flash many parts of their bodies on stage, especially as demanded by the roles of the Western women. It then occurred to me to get around the problem by re-invoking one of the oldest traditions of ancient Greek theatre: to cast men in some of the female roles'. This approach resulted in some criticism. According to El-Ramly, 'some critics and intellectuals complained that in showing the Western female activists in such a burlesque manner and clad in semi-nude dresses I was, in effect, confirming the stereotype of the licentious West already strong in the Egyptian spectator's imagination' (El-Ramly 2005a, 2005b). El-Ramly delights in overturning narrow interpretations and exposing limited ideologies, commenting that it was a pity that the (justified) criticism of the invasion of Iraq had not been accompanied by an equally strenuous denunciation of the practices of Saddam's regime. Ironically, since the execution of Saddam the play has not been restaged and its impact on spectators in the Arab world (and elsewhere) would probably be coloured by changes in attitude to Sadaam in the light of subsequent events in Iraq.

The Egyptian academic and theatre critic for *Al Ahram*, Professor Nehad Selaiha, who was initially critical of Koztamani's *Lysistrata* writing project as she thought it underestimated the existing substantial and close connection between theatre and contemporary politics in the Arabic theatre of the Mediterranean region, has written a detailed account of the 2004 production. She describes how the play began with a 'deceptively light-hearted choral prologue (on the model of the Greek *parabasis*), in which the Chorus of men and women, dressed in an approximation of the ancient Greek style ... warn us that they are all amateurs, with no stars in the case, tell us that the play is a disputatious parody of *Lysistrata*, deny that it

87

has any political message and disclaim any responsibility for it should it fail to please us'.

Then the mood changes and the play includes a new scene in which a woman sits alone, silently reading a letter while extracts from the work of the canonical Iraqi poet Abdel Wahab El-Bayati are sung to represent what she is reading – a nostalgic love letter from her husband who has fled from the terror of Saddam's regime. She is Labiba (the wise one) and the modern counterpart of Lysistrata. Subsequently the play follows Aristophanes' play quite closely for two-thirds of its length. Only in the final third does it veer away from the Aristophanic formula and address the present. The peace advocates' alliance fragments. The Western women leave; the Iraqi women are sent back to the traditional private spheres of the home; the chaste virgin prepares to blow herself up, calling this her wedding night. The soundscape of sirens, explosions and aircraft noise takes over.

Selaiha characterises El Ramly's production as 'a savagely ironic, intertextual engagement with Aristophanes' *Lysistrata* across the gap of centuries, where the scene becomes Baghdad and the time immediately before the American invasion. In this new setting, the recalcitrant ideological issues underpinning the conflict between a predominately Muslim Arab world and a predominately Christian West are ruthlessly bared and made to destroy the solidarity of women … [The play] depicts a bereaved nation, exhausted by the war with Iran, disgusted with the massacre of the Kurds in the north, straining under the weight of an oppressive, dictatorial military regime, wearied and depleted by the economic sanctions, and trembling at the prospect of yet another devastating war and more destruction. The Hellenic plot of Athenian, Spartan, Corinthian and Boiotian women to stop the war by staging a sex-strike in their respective territories is replayed by Iraqi and Western women from the States, Britain, France and Germany.'

El-Ramly has recounted the reaction of one Western long-term resident in Egypt: 'This time you have not left anyone unscathed: the East and the West alike' (El-Ramly 2005a, 177). He sees comedy as 'an exemplary way of transcending all differences … laughter arises out of the sincere depiction of truth, albeit through the use of the imagined and the improbable'. Comedy can also be closely related to tragedy – 'after all, tragedy is but the dark canvas against which the entire colours of comedy shine and disperse'. The Lysistrata Project, Kotzamani's project with Arab writers and El-Ramly's play and its critical reception bring this relationship between tragedy and comedy into an agonising tension.

References

Blume, Kathryn, 'Lysistrata Project', see http://www.kathrynblume. com/LysProj.htm and http://aquapiofilms.com/lys01.html

El-Ramly, Lenin (2005a), 'Comedy in the East and The Art of Cunning', in M. Kolk (ed.), *The Performance of the Comic in Arabic Theater, Documenta* XXlll.3, Gent, pp 166-80.

El-Ramly, Lenin (2005b), 'The Comedy of the East', tr. Hazem Azmy in *Ecumenica: a journal of theatre and performance* (www. ecumenicajournal.org: accessed 27 August 2008).

Kotzamani, Marina (2005), 'Lysistrata Joins the Soviet Revolution: Aristophanes as Engaged Theatre', in J. Dillon and S. Wilmer (eds), *Rebel Women: Staging Ancient Greek Drama Today* (London: Methuen), 78-111.

Kotzamani, Marina (2007), 'Lysistrata on Arabic Stages', *Performing Arts Journal* 83, 13-41.

Orfanos, Charalampos (2007), 'Revolutionary Aristophanes?' in E. Hall and A. Wrigley (eds), *Aristophanes in Performance, 421 BC-AD 2007* (Oxford: Legenda), 106-16.

Selaiha, Nehad, 'Lysistrata in Iraq', http://weekly.ahram.org.eg/ 2005/724/cu4.htm

I owe special thanks to Hazem Azmy and Marina Kotzamani for their generosity in providing information and discussion.

Lysistrata, or Loose Strife
A modern version by
David Stuttard
after Aristophanes

Characters of the Drama (in order of appearance)

Lucy (aka Lysistrata)	Leader of the Athenian Women's Resistance to the War
Nikki (aka Calonike)	Lysistrata's right-hand woman
Fanny (aka Myrrhine)	A yummy mummy
Claire (aka Lampito)	A rather butch lady from Sparta
Chorus of Old Men	Pompous frail geriatrics, proud of their past military prowess
Chorus of Old Women	Formidable and feisty grandmothers
Magistrate (aka Proboulos)	A harassed and incompetent civil servant
Dick (aka Cinesias)	Fanny's husband
Spartan Ambassador	A priapic gentleman
Molly Fication	A stunning naked girl, the personification of Reconciliation

1st and 2nd Hoodies
1st and 2nd Diners
Doorkeeper
Sundry other non-speaking
characters and musicians

Early morning. A street of houses giving onto a square. A door opens. Enter Lucy. *She is the most (apparently) demure of all the women we will meet, classy, as if she had been educated somewhere like Roedean.*

Lucy *I* don't know! If it had been some club or bacchic rave I'd invited them along to – something trendy like The Big Red Chilli or The Red Hot W...Whatever – if I'd asked them to come to something like that, the place would be heaving with handbags and hairspray! But look at it! Not a woman in sight. Except ... Wait a minute – here's my next-door neighbour. Morning, Nikki!

A second door opens. Enter Nikki, *a feisty woman.*

Nikki Morning, Luce. What's up with *you*? Oh, sweetheart, you need to take things easier, you do ... Look at you, you've got a face like thunder!

Lucy I'm absolutely furious. I mean, men keep on going on about how we women are so good for nothing ...

Nikki Well, they're right, dear.

Lucy ... and now I've asked them all to come round here for a *REALLY IMPORTANT DISCUSSION* and where are they? Still in bed. Not here, at any rate!

Nikki Don't worry, darling, they'll be here. You know how hard it is for women to get out the house. If it's not the husband, it's the nanny or the kids – putting them to bed, or washing them, or feeding them ... You know how it is!

Lucy But there's more to life than that – much more important things ...

Nikki Lucy, darling – what's with the mystery? Why have you asked us all round to yours? Is it something big?

Lucy Yes, very big.

Nikki And hard?

Lucy Yes, very hard.

Nikki And juicy?

Lucy Very very juicy, yes.

Nikki So what are we waiting for? Bring it on!!!

Lucy No, not that kind of something big and hard and juicy! Talk about a one-track mind! You're right, though. They'd have had no problem coming if it *had* been that!!! No, I've hit on something, and it's been keeping me awake at night, tossing and turning and tossing and turning and ...

Nikki Something delicate you can't quite put your finger on?

Lucy Something delicate, yes, but so, so simple. You see, we women have our country's future in our hands.

Nikki Our cunt ...? In our ha ...? We women? Not much hope there, then!

Lucy Our very existence is in our hands. Either the Spartans are wiped out ...

Nikki Good idea!

Lucy or the Thebans ...

Nikki Yes, I'm liking it a lot.

Lucy And as for Athens, well, I shan't even speak of it in case

94

it makes it come true. You know what I'm saying, though. But if we women all get together here, now – all the Theban women and the Spartan women, and us too – if we all get together now, united, we can save Greece.

Nikki Oh, yeah – like you expect us women to come up with some smart idea or something 'prudent', when all that most of us are interested in's the latest way to do our hair, or wear our mini party-dress or do our make-up, or maybe sport a sexy cocktail dress with strappy high-heeled shoes …

Lucy Yup, you've got it. That's how we'll save Greece. With our mini party-dresses and our perfume and our make-up and our sheer lingerie and sexy heels …

Nikki But how?

Lucy So that from today no man will raise his weapon in anger against another …

Nikki Raise his weapon? I'm getting my party-dress right now!

Lucy … or need protection …

Nikki Need protection? Make that my sexy cocktail dress!

Lucy … nor grapple hand-to-hand.

Nikki Bring on the high-heels! I could do with some grappling.

Lucy So where *are* all the women?!

Nikki They should have *definitely* got here – couldn't they have clubbed together and got a taxi?

Lucy They're Greeks – everything they do, they do late. And everything takes so long – starting, finishing, coming, g…

Nikki Sometimes I wish my husband was a bit more like that!

Lucy I thought at least the women from Acharnia would have got here by now – they live only just down the road!

Nikki There's a good few pubs on that road, though. But look! There's someone coming now!

Lucy And look there – look, there's more!

Nikki Fantastic! Look! Where are *they* from?

Lucy Anageeros.

Nikki Anna who? Well, geeros, schmeeros, bring on the beer-os …

Enter Fanny, *young and sexy, from down the road.*

Fanny I'm not late am I, Luce? What? What's with the silence?

Lucy Fanny! I don't think much to people who can't be bothered getting here on time for something so important.

Fanny Can't be bothered? I only just managed to find my knickers, it was so dark when I got up. Look, if it's so important, we're here now – tell us what it's all about.

Nikki No, hang on – wait a bit – the Theban women and the Spartans are arriving.

Lucy That's more like it. Look – there's Claire.

Enter Claire, *a somewhat masculine lady, possibly sporting short hair and tattoos. She is accompanied by three shy but shapely girls.*

Lucy My dearest Claire, sweet Spartan sister – you're looking lovely, very lovely, very sweet – and healthy, well-toned – you look like you could throttle a bull with your bare hands!

Claire Spend a lot of time at the gym. Pelvic thrusts.

Nikki God, I wish I had breasts like yours.

Claire Whatcha think you're doing? Not a piece of meat, you know.

Lucy And this other young lady – where's she from?

Claire Classy, she is. Theban.

Nikki Little cunt-ry girl, is she? I bet her meadow's nicely mown ...

Lucy And this other girl?

Claire From Chios. And this one here's from Corinth.

Lucy From Chios? Like the wine? Appropriately full-bodied.

Claire Whose idea was it to get us all together, then?

Lucy Mine.

Claire Well, go on – say what you want to say.

Nikki Yes, go on, dear – tell us what you think is so important.

Lucy All right, then. But before I do – a question. One small teensy-weensy question.

Nikki Whatever.

Lucy (*with total seriousness of purpose*) Don't you miss your husbands – don't you miss the fathers of your children, serving at the front so far from home? Don't think that I don't know. Don't think that I don't understand. Every woman here – her husband's overseas.

Nikki Mine's been away five months now.

Fanny Mine seven.

Claire If I do see mine, it's just a lightning visit to service his equipment – in and out before I know it.

Lucy And never mind our husbands – what about our lovers! All gone – all of them! No one left to give us succour. And what with the most recent disaster and the leather trade drying up, you can't get a decent twelve-inch dildo for love or money. So what would you say if I'd come up with a plan – would you join with me to end the war?

Nikki God, yes! Definitely! Even if I had to strip off naked and get drunk this very minute!

Fanny Me too – even if I had to cut myself in two like a ... *(already running out of imagery)* like a fillet of flatfish on the fish counter and ... and ... give half of myself away ... *(by now rather sheepish)* me too!

Claire And me – I'd go back home and climb the highest mountain if I could see peace again.

Lucy Excellent! Well, here's the plan. No need for any more secrecy. Ladies, all we have to do, to force our husbands to make peace, is give up ...

Nikki What? What? Tell us!!!

Lucy You'll do it?

Nikki Even if we die in the attempt!

Lucy Really? You will? You promise?

Nikki To get my hands on a twelve-inch dildo again? I'd do anything!

Lucy Sex. We've got to give up sex.

The women *begin to leave the stage, shaking their heads, some perhaps exclaiming 'No way!' or 'You must be joking!'*

Lucy Hey! What do you think you're doing? Where are you going? Don't tut at me! And don't look like that either! Blushing, crying ... Will you do it or not? Look, what's stopping you?

Nikki I just couldn't. That's all. The war must go on!

Fanny I couldn't either. God no, not sex! And so ... the war must go on!

Lucy You're the one who said you'd cut yourself in half, flatfish!

Nikki Look, whatever ... I'd walk through fire if I had to. Anything but give up sex. There's just nothing like it, Luce.

Lucy *(to* Fanny*)* And you?

Fanny I vote for the fire-walk.

Lucy Frailty, thy name is woman! Those playwrights have got us just about summed up – have our own way and bugger the consequences. *(to* Claire, *seductively)* But you, sweet Spartan sister – you're still with me, aren't you? And between us we can save the day. What do you say?

Claire Well, it's not easy for me to sleep alone without my Willy in bed with me. But as things stand ... We must have peace!

Lucy You absolute brick! You're the only real woman here!

Nikki Look – if ... just supposing ... we did give up ... you know ... what you were saying – and I really hope it never comes

99

to it – but if we did, what difference would it make? How would it help to end the war?

Lucy It would make all the difference! Look, say we're in the bedroom, nicely made-up, and naked – maybe a sexy negligée – a fresh bikini-wax: our husband's there, too, with a massive hard-on, gagging for a shag; what do we do? Not lie back with open … arms, no – cross our legs, say no, and no and no and what will happen? Before you know it, there'll be peace. I'm sure of it!

Claire They do say that when Menelaus saw Helen naked he threw down *his* sword.

Nikki But what if our husbands leave us?

Lucy A dog won't leave its bone.

Nikki A good boner's what I need! But what if they drag us into the bedroom and try to force themselves on us?

Lucy Stop them from getting in!

Nikki But if they make us do it?

Lucy Just make sure the sex is really bad – and make it obvious you're really not into it. It doesn't do it for them if think you're not enjoying it. And anyway, the point is that *they* mustn't enjoy it. They'll stop soon enough if you don't respond. A man's ego's never satisfied unless he thinks he's giving his woman pleasure.

Nikki *(to* Lucy *and* Claire*)* Well, if you both think that's a good plan … I second it!

Claire We'll force our husbands to make a just and fair peace. But I don't know how you're going to get your average Athenian chav-on-the-street to see sense.

Lucy Leave that to us.

Claire But your navy's in such good shape – and your defence budget's massive.

Lucy All taken care of. We're going to seize the treasury *today*. While we're in charge of titivation, so to speak, the more senior among us have been assigned the duty of occupying the treasury – they're getting in undercover, pretending they're on a pensioners' outing.

Claire Good work! You've got it all thought out.

Lucy So, Claire, what do you say? Shall we get on with it and seal our alliance with an oath?

Claire Give us the oath. We'll swear it.

Lucy Well said! Where's the registrar?

The Registrar *steps forward.*

Lucy *(to* Nikki*)* What are you looking at? *(to the* Registrar*)* Place your weapon on the ground and hand me the necessary.

The Registrar *places her weapon (perhaps a pistol) on the ground and hands Lucy a book on which to take the oath.*

Nikki *(sceptically)* Lucy – what oath are you going to make us swear?

Lucy The one which, in the words of the great poet, will make us 'screw our courage to the sticking place'.

Nikki But, Luce, if this is an oath about peace, why are we saying it over a weapon?

Lucy What do you want us to do, then? Sacrifice a white bullock or something?

Nikki No – bollocks to bullocks.

Lucy So, what do you suggest?

Nikki I'll tell you. We get a great big demijohn of wine – the best and strongest wine known to humanity – upend it, and swear an oath together that we'll never ... drink water again!

Claire That's certainly a good oath!

Lucy Bring on the demijohn!

In disgust, the Registrar *picks up her weapon and departs. Meanwhile another* woman *drags on a huge demijohn of wine.*

Nikki Just look at that! It gives you pleasure just to see it!

Lucy Set it down there, and raise the swine – I mean the wine – on high. Mistress Persuasion, and thou most dearest wine glass, receive this our sacrifice most graciously from our womanly hands.

They pour out a pint glass of wine. As they do so, the conversation continues.

Nikki It's got a good colour – and doesn't it pour well?!

Claire Nice bouquet – good nose ...

Nikki Ladies, let me be the first to swear.

Fanny No, no, no – the order must be chosen by lot.

Lucy Claire – let every woman place her right hand on the wine-cup and one of you repeat after me – the rest of you will subsequently swear to uphold the oath. Ready? Okay. I swear I shall allow no man, either lover nor husband ...

Nikki I swear I shall allow no man, either lover nor husband ...

Lucy ... to come near me with a hard-on.

Nikki ... to come near me with a hard-on. Oh, Luce, I'm feeling faint already!

Lucy I'll behave like a nun ...

Nikki I'll behave like a nun ...

Lucy ... though looking like a whore ...

Nikki ... though looking like a whore ...

Lucy ... until my man is crazy with desire for me ...

Nikki ... until my man is crazy with desire for me ...

Lucy ... and I'll never give myself to him willingly ...

Nikki ... and I'll never give myself to him willingly ...

Lucy ... but if he forces himself upon me ...

Nikki ... but if he forces himself upon me ...

Lucy ... I'll act all huffy, and I'll lie there like a block of ice.

Nikki ... I'll act all huffy, and I'll lie there like a block of ice.

Lucy I'll never wrap my legs around him ...

Nikki I'll never wrap my legs around him ...

Lucy ... or do it doggy-fashion.

Nikki ... or do it doggy-fashion.

Lucy In drinking this wine, I agree to this oath ...

Nikki In drinking this wine, I agree to this oath ...

Lucy ... and if I break my oath, I shall hereafter drink nothing but water.

Nikki ... and if I break my oath, I shall hereafter drink nothing but water.

Lucy Do you all likewise swear?

All We do.

Lucy Give me that wine-cup! (*She takes a small sip.*)

Nikki That's enough, dear! You need to leave some for us – we're all allies now!

Claire (*Hearing noises off.*) What's that noise?

Lucy It's like I said. The women have seized the treasury. Claire – go home and see to everything there. But leave these other women here as security. And we'll go to the treasury and man the barricades!

Nikki But won't the men come out in force as soon as they hear?

Lucy (*Acting cool, for effect.*) Do I look like I'm bothered? There's only one thing they can do to get us to open our gates – and that's accept our conditions.

Nikki Absolutely!!! We'll show them just how right they were when they said hell hath no fury like a woman!

Exeunt all women. *Immediately, the* Chorus of Old Men *enters. They are all ludicrous caricatures, rather like the Major in* Fawlty Towers, *dressed in shabby and vaguely military costume, perhaps wearing medals, some weighted down with massive burdens of damply smouldering wood, some with smoky*

104

braziers. Except where shown, the lines should be spoken by individuals.

Old Men Come on, old fellow. Keep on going. God, but this wood we're carrying is heavy! I feel just like we're those chappies in that play we did at school – something Scottish about Birnam Wood. Never did see the point in it.

Well, that's life, but who'd have thought it?
Who'd have thought the little women
we've been nurturing in our homes
would have turned out so rebellious,
independent, ill-disposed,
barricading the exchequer,
occupying the treasury,
annexing all we hold sacred,
all their entrances tight closed!

Come on, that's enough of that – let's get to the city as quickly as we can! We'll circle them and smoke them out. And we'll put the ringleaders on a bonfire, all of them, condemned by one vote, and we'll burn the lot of them. Let's start with Anne Robinson.*

They're not going to make a laughing-stock of me! Oh no, not as long as I've got anything to do with it.

Johnny foreigner tried to defeat us
with his Luftwaffe and blitz
but we rallied round defiant
and we stopped the little Fritz
and we fought them on the beaches
and we fought them on the seas
and we kicked their foreign arses
and we brought them to their knees.

I didn't fight so this would happen,
so society would fail,

*Substitute the name of a current female politician or celebrity as desired.

so we'd be ruled by yobs and women
who don't read the *Daily Mail*!
No. Forget the p.c. claptrap
that the woolly liberals peddle!
Let's restore some law and order
or I'm giving back my medal.

God, but it's a steep road –
least you know you're still alive,
though I don't know why we're walking –
so much easier to drive.
But the journey must be taken
and flame must be kept lit.
If it's gone out when we get there
we'll all be in deepest shit.

(All together) Oh, the smoke, the smoke,
the smokey smokey smoke!

And I can't see where I'm going
and I can't see where to go
and my eyes feel like two yellow
pools of dog-piss in the snow.

(All together) But we must march on
we must march on
we must march on
to save
        the city
And we must march on
we must march on
we must march on
to save
        the day

(All together) through the smoke, the smoke,
the smokey smokey smoke!

Oh, look – thank God for that! It's still alight!

During the speech which follows, they form a circle round the braziers, and place the wood into them. As the prayer is made, they stand to attention, remaining as a tableau as the Old Women *enter.*

Old Men Right-ho! Now, to begin with, let's position the wood here. Then we insert our pricks, I mean dicks, I mean sticks into these brassieres, I mean braziers, and when we're fully cocked we approach the women's front entrance and try and get inside. And if, despite our reasonable requests, the women still won't let us in, we give our pricks a quick blow job..., I mean we blow out the flames from our dicks..., I mean sticks, create a lot of smoke and smoke out the lot of them! So, let's bring ourselves off... I mean, unload ourselves. God, the smoke! Where's the army when you need it? Fat lot of good they are to us in Helmand*! That's better. Now to insert my pole and light my fire. O Lady Victory, grant that in the struggle with our women we might come off on top, in recognition of which we vow to erect a massive column in your honour, amen.

Enter Chorus of Old Women – *as much caricatures as the* Old Men *and as ludicrous. They are all carrying jugs or pails of water.*

Old Women I'm sure I can smell smoke, you know. I'm sure there's something burning. Come on, let's go and investigate.

Quick, come quick, Victoria,
before we're all burned into cinders
by these geriatric boy scouts
and their bonfires. And the wind is
veering round towards us –
I'm afraid there'll be great slaughter
if we don't do something quickly.
Drench the old gits in cold water!

---

*Substitute the location of a current military campaign as desired.

I'm coming, dear – I've got some water here for you. Look – what do you think of these jugs. Are they big enough, do you think?

Just look at all those ghastly codgers'
Psyched up like they're on campaign –
Arm-chair generals with zimmers!
But we'll turn them back again!

Come on, granddad,
come and get us,
come and put away your wrath!
Use your fire
to heat our water –
smells like you could use a bath!

Athene, goddess, we beseech you,
grant to us a safe release!
All we want's to stop the war
and save our city and all Greece!
Be our ally, our protectress.
Save us as you'd save a daughter.
Keep us safe and keep us fire-proof
Drench the old gits in cold water!

(*to the* Old Men) Right, that's enough. What's going on here? You should all be ashamed of yourselves! I never thought I'd live to see respectable old men like you behaving like young louts!

The Old Men *cease their tableau and confront the* Old Women.

Old Man   Well, who'd have thought it? I can't believe my eyes! A swarm of women coming pouring out as reinforcements!

Old Woman   What's up with you, then? Scared of being outnumbered? Just wait until you see how many more of us there's still to come!

Old Man I say, old man, are we going to let them prattle on? A good seeing to with our rods is what they need!

Old Woman Jugs on the ground, ladies! Don't want to be encumbered if it comes to hand to hand!

Old Man What's the delay, chaps? Knock 'em about a bit – they'll soon be quiet!

Old Woman Go on, then – try it! But let me warn you, if you do, you can kiss your balls goodbye!

Old Man If you don't shut up, I'm going to turn you inside out!

Old Woman If you touch even the tip of my little finger ...

Old Man Go on! What then? What if you feel my fists, what then? Nothing *you* can do can frighten *me*!

Old Woman *(dramatically)* I'll tear your flesh to pieces with my teeth and glut my hunger on your guts and lungs.

Old Man You know – Euripides was right! There *is* no creature crueller than a woman!

Old Woman *(as a military order, like 'Present arms')* Present jugs!

With military precision, the Old Women *pick up their jugs and pails.*

Old Man What do you think you're doing coming here with all that water anyway?

Old Woman And what are you old tombstones doing with that fire? Getting ready for your own cremation?

Old Man It's going to be your funeral, not ours!

Old Woman Not if we've got anything to do with it! That's where the water comes in!

Old Man How?

Old Woman You'll find out soon enough!

Old Man The only question is – am I within range to give you a good roasting?

Old Woman You don't by any chance have soap with you, do you? It'll come in handy for your bath!

Old Man A bath? For me? It's you that smells of fish!

Old Woman Call it a bridal shower!

Old Man *(blustering and outraged)* Did you hear what she just said?

Old Woman It's called free speech!

Old Man It'll be free shrieks of pain in a minute from *you*!

Old Woman Shame you won't be around any more to draw your pension!

Old Man Set fire to their hair!

Shambolically, the Old Men *wave their smoky sticks.*

Old Women Jugs – to action!

With a precise, almost military movement, the front rank of Old Women *throw the water from their jugs and pails at the* Old Men.

Old Men *(yelping as they are drenched with water)*

110

Old Woman Nice and hot, was it?

Old Men *(severally)* What do you mean? It's freezing! No! Stop! Stop! What are you doing?

The second rank of Old Women *repeat the water-throwing action.*

Old Woman Just watering you to make you grow!

Old Man I'm getting a fever – I'm shaking like a leaf!

Old Woman Why don't you warm yourself up with your fire, then?

During the last encounter, the scene has changed to represent the outside of a pair of massive doors set into a wall with a walkway at the top of it. Enter a pompous Athenian Magistrate.

Magistrate Right! That's enough! Women, eh? Always going on your little marches, with your placards and your drums, 'stop this', 'stop that', 'ban the next thing' … I remember – start of the war – chaps having an orderly debate in parliament. And what happened? Just before the vote about sending out our task force, woman in the gallery starts wailing something about sending our sons to war without the right equipment.

Same thing happened when we had the vote on sending troops to … can't remember where. Different woman this time – drunk, I think – starts groaning on about how we'd kill innocent civilians. Sentimental tosh like that. Anyway, the minister kept going, like he always does, the old fool. Never does know when to stop. But these women, they … they always go too far.

Old Man You don't know the half of it. Their previous behaviour was bad enough, but they've gone and emptied vats of water over us. Completely drenched us! Looks as if we've pissed ourselves!

111

Magistrate Our fault really. Been far too complicit. Given them their heads. Let them get ideas above their station.

Say we're at the jewellers, 'Jeweller,' we say, 'necklace you repaired for me? – other evening, little woman out dancing, pin thing slipped out of its clasp. Got to go away on business. Wondered, if you've time, if you could go round to my house tonight and fit the chappie snugly in the hole?'

Or say you're at the cobblers, some young chap with a great big ... what do you call it? ... anyway, you say, 'Cobbler chappie, little woman's sandal – strap thing too tight, chaffing her toe. Delicate young thing. Could you pop round with your what-do-you-call it later on this afternoon and see what you can do to open up the aperture a bit?' And what thanks do we get?

Top civil servant. Just secured a deal to buy munitions on the cheap, come round to the treasury to sort out the finances. What do I find? Can't get in. And why? These women.

But no point standing about talking. Get some crowbars, snappish. Going to teach them all a lesson. What you gawping at, you fool? And you, what are you staring at? Think you're at the theatre?

He gives a crowbar to one of the Old Men*, who places it at the bottom of the door and starts straining to try to open it.*

Now, look, you put the tip down here like this, down at the bottom here, like this, and give it a good heave-ho – no, not like that. No, let me show you. Tip to bottom, here, like this, and heave and ho and ...

He takes the crowbar and, starts heaving with it, his hips moving in a very suggestive manner. The door opens suddenly, sending the Magistrate *sprawling. Enter* Lucy

112

Lucy No need for that. Look, here I am, outside, and voluntarily. What are you doing with all that *materiel*? That's where you're going wrong. It's not *materiel* you need, but intelligence and diplomacy.

Magistrate And what do you know about it? You're a hooligan! Where's security? Place her under arrest. Cuff her hands behind her back.

Lucy If he so much as touches me – and I don't care who he is – he'll regret it.

Magistrate *(to* Old Men*)* You're not frightened, are you? Look – you seize her round the waist, and you put the handcuffs on!

Enter Nikki. *She takes up a threatening position in front of one section of* Old Men.

Nikki If you lay a finger on her, we women will retaliate so hard you'll shit yourself so much you'll drown in it!

Magistrate I won't be spoken to like that! Another member of security here, now! Arrest *her* first and gag her!

Enter Fanny. *She too takes up a threatening position in front of some other* Old Men.

Fanny If you so much as harm a hair of her head, you'll be straight to A&E before you know it!

Magistrate Right, that's enough! Security! Get that one! Do this methodically, we'll stop them!

Enter Claire. *She threatens the remaining* Old Men.

Claire Harm her in any way, I'll pull your hair out by the roots – and not your head hair either! Bring tears to your eyes, *that* will!

Magistrate Bloody hell! I'm out of men! Mustn't let them win, though! Can't have that! Into formation, men – we're going to attack!

Lucy It's only fair to let you know that inside there's four regiments of monstrous women, all armed to the teeth!

Magistrate Arrest them, men!

For a moment, the Old Men *hesitate.*

Lucy *(calling for reinforcements from inside)* Ladies of the common cause, come forth now! Ballerinas, hotel cleaners, rich high flyers, fast-food fryers, breast enhancers and pole dancers, barmaids, housemaids, nursemaids, milkmaids, black cab drivers, deep-sea divers, p.a.'s, d.j.'s, brides with bouquets, city slickers, tarts and vicars, good-time girls with tattooed tummies, dykes and grannies, yummy mummies, women of the world united, come forth now, your time has come! Kick 'em! Slap 'em! Up and at 'em! Use your fingernails and fight! Make them bowed and cowed and bloodied! Women of the world unite!

Women pour out onto the stage, joining the Old Women. *They attack the men and, in a highly stylised and choreographed battle, easily defeat them. The men lie or sit around, dazed, on the stage.*

Lucy Cease fire! Fall back! We accept your surrender.

Magistrate I say, chaps! They've defeated us! Humiliated us !

Lucy What did you expect? That we were weak and fragile little girlies? That women don't have the balls to fight?

Magistrate Well, yes, as it happens. Yes. I thought the only thing that you had balls for was ... well ... balls. By which I mean parties, you see ... Dances ... That sort of thing.

Old Men
> They're just like animals, your honour!
> No point talking. Waste of breath!
> They've just soaked us in cold water –
> Freezing! Nearly caught my death!

Old Women
> Live and let live, that's our motto,
> Chaste and modest, sweet as pie.
> But if you try our patience too much
> You can kiss *your* balls goodbye!

Old Men *(gradually getting to their feet and dusting themselves off.)* This is insufferable! They're animals, the lot of them. Question them! Interrogate them! Use every trick in the book, if needs be. We must get to the bottom of all this. Why've they occupied the Treasury? You can't let them get away with it – too dangerous a precedent!

Magistrate First thing I want to know is why you've barricaded yourselves inside the Treasury. Treasury belongs to us, you know.

Lucy It's so that we can look after the Exchequer and so that money's no longer part of the equation of the war.

Magistrate You think this war's got anything to do with money?

Lucy Money, yes, and all the other sleaze and back-room deals. It's all that politicians think about! Defence procurements here, duck ponds there, cash for peerages there*! It's the only reason they keep the war going! But the money's in the Treasury, under our control, and you are not going to get your hands on it any longer!

Magistrate So, what are you going to do?

* Feel free to substitute references to whatever political scandal is current.

115

Lucy You haven't got it, have you? From now on, we're in charge of public spending.

Magistrate In charge of public spending?! You?!

Lucy What's so odd about that? You expect us to be in charge of the housekeeping money at home, don't you? Or are you telling me that you don't leave it to your wife to check through the bank statements when they come, or pay the phone bill, or sort out the overdraft? And what do you say to her then? I can hear you now: 'You do it, darling! You're so much better at that sort of thing than I am!'

Magistrate But it's not the same thing!

Lucy How not?

Magistrate This is to do with war!

Lucy But there shouldn't *be* a war in the first place!

Magistrate How else can we protect ourselves?

Lucy We'll protect you!

Magistrate You?

Lucy Yes, us!

Magistrate You're mad!

Lucy But we'll protect you nonetheless – with or without your cooperation.

Magistrate This is outrageous!

Lucy You can bluster all you want! But that's how it is.

Magistrate It's illegal! It's unconstitutional!

Lucy   Look, relax! We'll *protect* you!

Magistrate   What if I don't want you to?

Lucy   That's all the more reason why we should!

Magistrate   *(trying to be conciliatory)* Whatever put this notion that you knew anything about war and peace into your pretty little head?

Lucy   That's what we're going to explain to you.

Magistrate   *(close to losing his temper)* Well just hurry up and do it, then, before I rearrange that smug bloody face of yours!

Lucy   Just listen, then, and try if you can to control yourself. Think of your blood pressure!

Magistrate   My blood pressure! Damn my bloody blood pressure!

Nikki   It'll be your funeral!

Magistrate   If anyone croaks, it'll be you, you old hag! *(to* Lucy*)* Speak!

Lucy   Alright, I will. In the first phase of this war, we showed the restraint which is characteristic of the female sex, and we supported our husbands in all they did. In point of fact, you didn't give us much option – we certainly didn't agree with you! Oh no, we knew very well what you were up to! News was always filtering home about how badly you were handling the war. And I was worried – I didn't like it. But all I could do when my husband came home was smile sweetly and say: 'What resolutions were passed today, then, dear – anything about peace-talks?' and all *he* could do was say it was none of my bloody business and tell me to shut up. So I *did* shut up.

Nikki I wouldn't have shut up!

Magistrate You'd have had your face rearranged if you hadn't!

Lucy Well, I *did* shut up. And things went from bad to worse. And if I asked my husband how anyone could make such a mess of things, he'd look at me in that patronising way of his and tell me if I didn't keep my mouth shut, he'd give me the blackest eye that anyone had ever seen. And then he'd strike a pose and put the patriotic music on and go on about how 'we shall fight on the beaches, we shall fight on the landing grounds, we shall fight in the fields and in the streets, we shall fight in the hills; we shall never surrender'!

Magistrate Good man! Jolly well said!

Lucy No, not jolly well said at all! Jolly stupidly said! And when we realised there wasn't one man on any of the warring sides who had an ounce of sense, we women knew we had to join together to save Greece. What was the good of just sitting back and expecting things to happen? And now, if you'd keep quiet and just listen when *we* speak, like you expect us to listen to you, we'd sort the whole thing out!

Magistrate Listen to you? This is insufferable! You just don't know what you're talking about!

Lucy Enough!

Magistrate Enough?!!! You're telling me 'enough'? Look, just keep out of it. All you women know about is hoovering and dusting and crocheting and knitting and ... and make-up and ... and ...

Lucy Feeling left out, are we? Well, that's easy fixed.

At Lucy's *signal, the women start to apply make-up to the* Magistrate.

Lucy

A little bit of blusher and a little bit of lippy
Some mascara and some eyeliner –
Now, keep your big mouth zippy!

Nikki

And here's some wool and needles
and the point of this charade is
that if men are ballsing up the war
just leave it to the ladies!

Old Women

Put down your tea-pots, make a stand!
The time to help our sisters is at hand!

Our fearless sisters, bold and beautiful and brave,
our peerless sisters, clever, passionate and pretty,
if dancing were the way to win the day,
I'd dance forever and I'd help them save the city!

So, grannies and young feisty mothers,
Think how these measly men maligned us!
Be bold now! Forward to the fight!
The day is ours! The wind's behind us!

Lucy If I'm right, if we've not lost our touch, if our breasts and legs and thighs are still as hot and horny as they always were, if they still bring out our men in hot sweats, straining their cocks stiff to bursting point to have us, then I think that Lucy's going to win the day and loosen Greece from the barbarities of war!

Magistrate What are you going to do?

Lucy To start with, stop you lot coming in full body-armour to our village sales.

Nikki God, yes – I second that!

119

Lucy You can't move for tripping over soldiers jamming up the home-produce stalls.

Magistrate Brave boys those – takes courage to face the Women's Institute!

Lucy But some guy brisling with weaponry haggling at the cheese counter – it's ridiculous!

Nikki I saw one the other day – lovely young man with such nice hair – a cheese pastry, nowhere to put it, hides it underneath his helmet. And then there was that other one, big strapping boy – he comes in with his weapon in his hand, waving it about in front of everyone, and it was a big one too – well, my poor friend comes over all faint, and … what can a poor girl do? She doesn't really have a choice. She just lies there and lets him get away with everything he wants.

Magistrate But the situation on the ground is so confused – how could you *hope* to end the war?

Lucy Easily!

Magistrate How? Show me!

Lucy We women have to do it all the time with balls of wool, when the cat's got to our knitting – you know! You pull a bit here, you get out the knitting needles and you ease a bit here, you tweak a bit there … And that's how we'll end the war – with your permission – send out the diplomats, ease a bit here, tweak a bit there …

Magistrate So you mean to stop the war with balls of wool and knitting needles! You must be off your heads!

Lucy If you had any sense at all, you'd base all your policy on our balls of wool.

Magistrate How do you work that one out, then? Eh?

Lucy The first thing you do with wool, when it's straight off the sheep, is you put it in a big bath of water to get rid of the filth. Well, we've plenty of filth in this city that needs getting rid of! And next you stretch it on a frame and you pick off all the hangers-on and the impurities and then the ones that huddle stubbornly together, thick as thieves, or wind themselves about in old school ties so that it's only them that has the power – you prise them apart and you pick them off one by one. Now, when you have eliminated all the undesirables, you put the rest in one big pot – the pot of human decency – yes! everyone together: citizens, asylum-seekers, any friends abroad – yes, even any council-tax dodgers that have still escaped the mesh! And all the other countries, too – all must be gathered in, like wool caught on barbed-wire. And so you bring them in and put them all together, and from diversity you create a harmony, one great big ball of wool, and with that wool you clothe the people.

Magistrate This is outrageous! You sit here and speak of bits of thread and balls of wool, and yet you shoulder none of the responsibilities of war!

Lucy You sad, pathetic man! We shoulder the responsibilities of war two, three times more than you! For one thing, it is women who give birth to sons, women send their brave sons off to war …

Magistrate Enough! Don't open painful wounds!

Lucy And when we're still young enough that we can still enjoy our youth, we sleep alone – our husbands are off at the front. No more of that, though – think of the girls, who have no husbands, growing old alone in the cold single beds of their childhood!

Magistrate Men grow old, too.

Lucy But it is not the same! A man comes home. He has white hair. Bingo! He marries a teenager. But a woman has but a

121

little time, and if she does not use it well, well no one wants to marry her, and that's what breaks my heart!

Magistrate Well, absolutely – if a chap can still achieve a hard-on …

During the next short scene, the women cover the helpless Magistrate *with wreaths as if for his funeral.*

Lucy
It's your funeral, if you won't learn –
I'll pack your ashes in a Grecian urn –
I'll make the sandwiches and cake
And buy the flowers to celebrate your wake.

Nikki Look, here's a wreath

Fanny And here's some flowers

Lucy
And this scene could go on for hours.
But the hearse is here, the hearse can't wait,
We mustn't make the driver late.

Magistrate This is insupportable! You can't treat me like this! I'm going straight to the City Hall to tell them what you've done to me!

Lucy Oh, yes? And what's your complaint? That we've left something out? Don't worry – we'll make sure *The Times* prints your obituary. It'll be the most impressive column that you've ever had!

The Magistrate *is carried out to much merriment from the women.* Lucy, Nikki, Fanny *and* Claire *leave the stage. The* Old Men *and* Old Women *are ranked on either side of the stage. In what follows, they draw up their battle lines again. Each section is spoken individually by different members of the choruses.*

Old Men   Right, that's it! No time to lose! Chaps, it's a crisis!
Action stations, now!

I've got a nose for fishy business,
I can smell a rat,
A great big fishy rat, at that,
In fact, a coup d'état.

I'm sure the enemy's behind this,
Spreading mayhem, sowing tension
Using women as their spies to
Seize the Bank and steal my pension!

Women in government? Preposterous! What do they
know of strategy and defence procurements? And all this
wanting us to hold talks with the enemy – it's all so
unbelievably naïve! Thank God us chaps can see it for
what it is – a conspiracy to turn us into a dictatorship.
But they're not going to dictate to me. Oh, no. Not as long
as I can help it, not as long as we still have our courage
and our valour and our hearts of oak, our pluck, our will,
our Dunkirk spirit, all those qualities which make our
country great. And I shall stand full square with Raleigh,
Wellington and Churchill, a hero with the heroes of the
past. And I swear this oath, this solemn sacred oath: if
any woman should approach me ... I'll punch her bloody
lights out!

Old Women   If your mother was alive, she wouldn't recognise
you after we've finished with you! Ladies, let us divest ourselves of all impedimenta. (*They roll up their sleeves and
make themselves look threatening.*)

We love our city too, you know.
It's nurtured us, and more besides.
It let us join the brownies
And it let us join the guides.

We could have had a great career –
High salaries and high repute.
Instead we married and grew old
And joined the Women's Institute.

Should I not help my city in a time of crisis? Yes, I was born
a woman. Yes. But don't hold that against me – not if my
solution to the present crisis is more likely to succeed than
yours is. This is my country. Its men-folk are my children.
While you – you superannuated relics – what have you done
for Greece? You may have won the last war, but you lost the
peace. You lost the peace. You frittered everything away,
you squandered everything, and now you've brought us to
the brink of ruin. *(One of the* Old Men *shouts 'bollocks!')*
What's that? What did I hear you say? If you make me any
angrier, I swear I'll kick your smug old faces in!

Old Men I don't believe it! It's outrageous! Such behaviour!
And it's getting worse!

To the defence men!
Man the barricades and walls!
The time has come to show them
It's the men who have the balls!

So throw away your zimmers!
Throw away your walking sticks!
You may be old,
But you're still bold –
Remember your old tricks!

So barefoot, like the desert rats,
We'll fight our Alamein again.
We'll wear our wings like heroes.
We'll be glorious! We'll be men!

Make no concessions, or they'll stop at nothing. They'll
take their battle to the seas and to the air. They may be
women, but remember Boudicca! And take no prisoners!

124

Old Women I swear that if you get me going, I'll get you going too – home, defeated, tails between your legs.

So, ladies, strip for battle!
Fight them, red in tooth and claw!
Give them everything you've got now –
Give them shock and give them awe!

From now on, dream of your steak pies,
And your beer and fish and chips –
'Cos we'll send you to intensive care,
You'll spend your lives on drips.

As long as Claire's alive, we shall not fear you. As long as the little country girl from Thebes still guards her entrance safe, we shall endure. You have no power for all your blustering and all your resolutions. And your politicians? Hated. By the people here and everywhere. You say new threats require new laws, new measures, new restrictions. You know what we say? Bollocks! Crap! We've had enough! So no more laws, no more restrictions! You know the drill, girls – rugby-tackle time! And no holds barred!

Another highly stylised and well-choreographed battle ensues. Again, the women *rout the* men, *who exeunt in confusion. Enter* Lucy.

Old Women (*in mock-tragic style*) Mistress, queen, governatrix of our thoughts and deeds, why come you here, and with so beetling a brow?

Lucy (*continuing in the same style*) The deeds and feeble ways of wanton womankind depress me, and cause me to roam now hither and now thither.

Old Women What are you saying? What are you saying?

Lucy The truth. The truth.

Old Women What is this strange and terrifying thing? Tell us, your dear, dear friends.

Lucy No – no, to speak of it is shameful, yet to stay silent is too much for anyone.

Old Women Do not keep it from me, whatever it should be that troubles you.

Lucy Then I'll be brief. THE WOMEN ARE GAGGING FOR A SCREW!!!

Old Women My God!

Lucy What's God got to do with it? It's pure biology! I don't know how much longer I can force them to keep away from men. They keep on slipping though my fingers. I just came across one – she'd been scouring the walls and found a little hole which she was frantically working with her fingers, trying to get as deep in as possible. And then there was another sliding down a pole. And another said she was ready to give herself that minute to the enemy. And another was so close to getting herself away – she was standing on the walls, all set to toss herself off. Refused to come when I told her to. I swear, I had to take her in hand and bring her off myself. And the excuses that they're making to go home! Look – here's another. Hey – what's the hurry? Where do you think *you're* going?

Enter Woman A

Woman A I must get home. I left the washing in the machine – it'll go cheesy.

Lucy Well, let it! Come back here!

Woman A Just let me spread it on the bed – I'll come as quickly as I can.

126

Lucy You're not coming anywhere.

Woman A You mean, I've got to let it go all cheesy?

Lucy Yes.

Enter Woman B

Woman B Look, I'm in the middle of fixing the car. The engine – I need to strip it down ...

Lucy Not the old 'I'm fixing the car' routine again ...

Woman B Yes, and when I'm totally stripped down, and everything's well lubricated, I'll find a nice straight shaft, one that fits snugly, and I'll slot it in tightly, and ...

Lucy That's enough. If I let you go, they'll all want shafting.

Enter Woman C

Woman C You've got to let me get to hospital! I'm having such contractions!

Lucy More nonsense!

Woman C But my water's broken!

Lucy You weren't even pregnant yesterday!

Woman C Well, I am today. I've got to go, Luce! Please! I've got to get myself seen to!

Lucy What are you on about? What have you got in there? It's very hard.

Woman C Of course it's hard – it's a man-child!

Lucy A man-child? I see – a massive saucepan, you mean? I thought you said you were pregnant.

Woman C I am pregnant. I am! I am!!!

Lucy Well, why've you got that thing stuffed up your dress?

Woman C In case I don't make it in time and I need to have a water birth.

Lucy Well now I've heard it all! You're staying right here – and as for that saucepan, it'll come in handy as a christening font.

Woman C But I can't stay in the Treasury a moment longer – I swear I saw a snake in there.

Woman A Me, too – those city sparrows are killing me. I can't get any sleep for all their twittering.

Lucy Enough already! Look – you're gagging for your men. Well, don't you think they're gagging for you, too? I know how long and hard the nights can be. But stick in there, ladies, and endure a little longer. It's written in the stars that we shall overcome – if we don't tear ourselves apart first. There's been a prophecy.

Woman B A prophecy?

Lucy A prophecy.

Woman C What does it say?

Lucy Keep quiet, and I'll tell you. (*She tries desperately to make up something that will rhyme.*)

'When pussies congregate on rocks
And keep themselves away from cocks,
Then God will put an end to woe.
What was above shall be below ...'

128

Woman A Does that mean women can always be on top from now on?

Lucy
 'But if the pussies can't agree,
 And if they leave the Treasury,
 Then they will lose the world's respects ...
 And all will know they're slaves to sex.'

Woman C God, that's amazing! It's like incredible!

Lucy So don't weaken. No, endure. Come back inside. It would be shameful, ladies, to ignore the prophecy.

Exit Lucy. *Enter* Chorus of Old Men. *For the moment at least they are less hostile.*

Old Men
 When I was but a little lad
 I heard this story from my dad
 About a young man who was dreading
 What would happen at his wedding.

 So he ran off to the jungle
 Where he lived on all things fungal,
 Where he'd hunt, and where he'd roam.
 And he never did go home.

 Rather, he became a mystic,
 Self-contained, misogynistic.
 And now among wise men there ain't
 One who'd not have him as his patron saint.

Old Man Come here, darling, give us a kiss!

Old Woman That's one thing you'll just have to miss.

Old Man Come on! I want to squeeze your boobs!

Old Woman Your fly's undone. What hairy pubes!

Old Men
Nothing wrong with being hairy.
Shows you're not some hot-waxed fairy.
Every fighter who's been tough
Has possessed a fine man-muff.

Old Women
God, you're an almighty bore!
I've a story to match your
Story of your mystic chum.
And I heard my story from my mum.

Old Timon was a homeless vagrant
Who lived in bushes and did not smell fragrant.
He'd a face like thunder, as grotesque as sin,
And if he'd had a home he'd have let no man come in.

'Cos he hated men for their evil ways
And he hated them till his dying days.
And if he saw a man go by, he'd run off and take cover.
But with women it was different – 'cos he was a red-hot lover.

Old Women Do you want a good slapping?

Old Men *(with mock terror)* Oh no, no, please! I'm so frightened!

Old Women Or a good kicking?

Old Men You just want to hitch up your skirt and show me
your fanny!

Old Women
You'll never see my fanny,
Which, although I'm an old granny,
Is a fanny in a million
Neatly waxed in a Brazilian.

Exit Chorus of Old Men. Lucy and Fanny *appear high on the walls above the gates.*

Lucy Women! Quick! Come here! As quickly as you can!

Old Women What is it? Tell me! What's the matter?

Lucy A man! A man! I can see a man! Actually, to tell the truth, he's more like a giant walking hard-on than a man. Trust the old sex-drive to keep men on the straight and – well, he's definitely not narrow!

Old Women Who is he? Where is he?

Lucy He's coming this way!

Old Women Oh yes! Yes! Yes! I can see him!

Lucy Look! Does anyone know who he is?

Fanny Oh my God! It's my husband Dick!

Lucy Right – your mission is to stoke his fire, to lead him on, to tease him, please him every way you can without actually pleasuring him, to go through the whole A to Z of foreplay but to stop short of – well, you remember the oath we made earlier.

Fanny No worries. I know what to do.

Lucy I'll be assistant stoker, warm him up a bit. The rest of you – make yourselves scarce!

Exeunt all except Lucy. *Enter* Dick *in a state of some excitement.*

Dick For fuck's sake, I'm throbbing fit to burst, and I'm so stiff it's torture!

Lucy Stop! Who comes there?

131

Dick It's me.

Lucy A man?

Dick Of course I'm a bleeding man! Are you blind?!

Lucy You can't come inside.

Dick Says who?

Lucy I'm the barrier-control – the prophylactic.

Dick For God's sake – I want Fanny!

Lucy Fanny?

Dick Fanny, yes! My wife!

Lucy Your wife?

Dick Yes! I'm her husband, Dick!

Lucy Ah, Dick! I see! The famous Dick! She can't stop talking about you. It's always, Dick this, Dick that – Dick's always on her lips. She's always bigging you up. And if she's licking an ice-cream or sucking on a lollipop she'll sigh, 'Oh, God, I want my Dick!'

Dick Oh God …!

Lucy Oh, yes. And if we get onto talking about our husbands, do you know what your wife says? She says, 'I bet none of your men measures up to my Dick.'

Dick Go on, PLEASE!!! Get her for me!

Lucy And if I do? What will you do for me?

Dick Anything you want, my darling! Look, I've got what it takes. Just tell me what you want, and I'll give you one!

Lucy All right! I'll just go down … and get your wife.

Exit Lucy.

Dick And quickly! PLEASE!!! Life holds no satisfaction for me since she left the house. I hate going home! It's all just one big wasteland, all unwelcoming and sterile! And despite my appetite, there's nothing I can do with my meat to satisfy my hunger. As you can see – I'm one big hard on!

Fanny (*from inside, as if to* Lucy) I love him, I love him, I *do* love him! But he doesn't want my love. Don't make me go down to him!

Dick Oh, my sweetest, succulentest Fanny, baby! Why are you doing this? Come down to me now!

Fanny For God's sake, no! I won't!

Dick It's me, Fanny, me, me calling – won't you come down?

Fanny It's not because you really *want* me that you're calling!

Dick I don't want you!!!? I want you so much I could burst!

Fanny No! I'm going.

Dick No! No! Listen to your little child, your baby! (*dressing up his phallus to look like a baby*) Come on, now! Call for mummy! (*pretending to be the baby*) Mammy! Mammy!! MAMMY!!! (*to* Fanny) What's wrong with you? have you no pity for your little child, unwashed, unsuckled now for six whole days?

Fanny Oh yes – I pity him! Quite obviously his father's not been looking after him!

Dick   (*through clenched teeth*) Come down, bless you!, to your child!

Fanny   Oh! Such is motherhood! I must go down! What else can I do?

Enter Fanny.

Dick   She looks so much younger than I remember her, and she's looking at me so adoringly! All that haughtiness of hers and her standoffishness – ooh! – all they do is inflame my desire all the more!

Fanny   (*to the 'baby', in a baby voice*) Oh, my sweetest little babesy-wabesy, what a wicked daddy you've got. Here's a little kiss for you, yes – mummy's little sweetie! (*she slaps the top of* Dick's *phallus*)

Dick   You wretched, bloody woman, why are you doing this? Why are you listening to all those other women? You're making me suffer, and you're all miserable yourself!

Fanny   Don't lay a hand on me!

Dick   And everything at home – my things and yours – will you just let them go to rack and ruin?

Fanny   I couldn't care less.

Dick   You couldn't care less that the cats are running around unravelling your knitting?

Fanny   For God's sake, no!

Dick   And all this time the rites of Aphrodite haven't been performed once! Won't you come back home?

Fanny   For God's sake, no! Not till you sit down at the negotiating table and stop the war!

Dick Well, all right, if you'd like – we'll do that, too.

Fanny Well, all right, if you do, then I'll come home. But for the moment, I've sworn not to.

Dick But ... after all this time, you can at least sleep with me!

Fanny No – no I can't. But I'm not saying I don't love you.

Dick You *do* love me? Yes? Then why won't you sleep with me, Fanny, love?

Fanny Oh, you silly man! In front of the baby?

Dick God, no! Look! Just for you, I've got rid of the baby. (*he unwraps his phallus, revealing it to her*) Now – won't you sleep with me?

Fanny But, my poor love, where can we do it?

Dick Where? Here's good for me!

Fanny But I need to ... clean up a bit. You know?

Dick That's easy – there's a shower in my dressing-room.

Fanny And so, poor darling, must I break my oath?

Dick I'll take responsibility for that! Don't worry about your oath!

Fanny Okay – look – I'll get us a bed.

Dick No! Don't do that! The ground'll do us fine!

Fanny Good heavens, no! I know what you're like, but *I*'m not doing it on the ground.

Exit Fanny. *In the increasingly slapstick scene which follows, she keeps rushing off and on to bring in the various bedroom items referred to in her speeches.*

Dick   (*to audience*) You see? It's perfectly obvious she finds me irresistible!

Enter Fanny, *with camp-bed.*

Fanny   Look, here it is! You lie down there, and I'll take my clothes off! And yet – oh, damn! – I need to get a mattress!

Dick   A mattress? Why? Don't get one just for me!

Fanny   Good heavens, yes! It would be dreadful just to do it on the springs!

Dick   Give us a kiss!

Fanny   There!

Exit Fanny.

Dick   (*licking his lips noisily*) Come back quickly now!

Enter Fanny, *with mattress.*

Fanny   Look, here's the mattress! You lie down and I'll take my clothes off! And yet – oh, damn it! – you don't have a pillow!

Dick   But I don't *need* a pillow!

Fanny   Perhaps *you* don't, but *I* do!

Exit Fanny.

Dick   But my prick's all ready, like a fat man drooling for his supper!

Enter Fanny *with a pillow.*

Fanny Head up! Up you get! There, I've got everything we need!

Dick You certainly do! Come on, my little treasure!

Fanny I'm just undoing my bra. Remember now – don't go all limp on me ... about negotiating with the enemy for peace!

Dick For God's sake – I would rather die!

Fanny But you don't have a blanket!

Dick For God's sake! I don't *need* a sodding blanket! I just want to screw!

Fanny You will, don't worry! I won't be long!

Exit Fanny.

Dick That woman and her bed-clothes will drive me mad!

Enter Fanny, *with a blanket.*

Fanny Up you get!

Dick I've *got* it up!

Fanny Do you want me to rub some oil in?

Dick No, by Apollo, no I don't!

Fanny Oh yes, by Aphrodite, yes, yes, yes – whether you want it or not!

Exit Fanny.

Dick Oh Lord God Zeus! I hope she spills the lot!

Enter Fanny, *with a jar.*

Fanny Stretch out your … hand. Come on, now! Take it! Rub it in!

Dick I don't like the smell of this oil – it's just wasting time, and it's certainly not an aphrodisiac!

Fanny O silly me! I brought the fly repellant!

Dick That's great, that is! Just leave it, won't you?

Fanny No, don't be silly!

Exit Fanny.

Dick I hope whoever invented these so-called love-oils is rotting in hell!

Enter Fanny, *with a larger jar*

Fanny Here's a nice big jar.

Dick I've got something of my own that's nice and big! Come on! Don't be a tease! Get on the bed and don't go off again!

Fanny I'll do just that. I'm taking off my shoes. Oh, darling, do say you'll vote for peace! Promise?

Dick Yes, yes – I will. I promise!

Fanny *(triumphantly)* Yes!

Exit Fanny – *this time clearly she's not coming back.*

Dick She's doing my nut in! My wife – she's killing me! She's skinning me alive!

138

Oh God, I'm out of luck now!
I've got nobody to fuck now!
Just look how my wife's treated me –
She's only gone and cheated me!
I bet she's in there chuckling
'Cos baby still needs suckling.
But if my wife won't treasure me
I'll pay a tart to pleasure me.

Enter Chorus of Old Men.

Old Men

My dear old thing, she's licked you –
Not like that! – I mean, she's tricked you!
And I pity you, by God I do
'Cos now she's gone you've no one who
Will take your old chap in her hands,
Your balls, your shaft, your gleaming glans,
And time is running out for you –
Where will you get your morning screw?

Dick It's throbbing and it's twitching!

Old Men

It's her fault, that scheming bitch in
There, the cunning cheating little cow!

Dick She's sexy – and I want her now!

Old Men

She's a sexy little cock-tease
And my prayer for her is: 'God, please
Send a hurricane or twister
To snatch up our sexy sister,
Raise her high at your command
And drop her, open-legged, to land,
Aiming perfectly to lodge her
On my well-poised, well-primed todger.'

Enter the Spartan Ambassador, and his entourage, all in a state of some excitement.

Ambassador Who's in charge round here? I've come with news.

Enter Athenian Magistrate, by now similarly aroused.

Magistrate Is that a herald's staff – or are you just pleased to see me?

Ambassador I'm an ambassador, old boy. And I've come from Sparta for the peace talks.

Magistrate Which is why you're bulging with weaponry?

Ambassador No – no I'm not.

Magistrate So why are you bending over like that? Why are you pulling down your jacket? Are you suffering from swellings from the journey?

Ambassador This man's an idiot!

Magistrate Oh look, you naughty, naughty man, you've got a massive hard-on!

Ambassador Don't be absurd. You're clearly moronic.

Magistrate So what's that, then?

Ambassador It's my wand of office.

Magistrate Excellent. And look *(demonstrating his bloated phallus)*, here's mine. So now that we've established our credentials, man to man, so to speak, you can tell me straight. What's going on in Sparta?

Ambassador In Sparta and the allied states it's all the same

– balls ups, cock ups everywhere. Shambolic. What we need's a common cunt – I mean a common front.

Magistrate   So, this affliction – where's it come from? From thin air?

Ambassador   No. From shapely Claire, more like. She and every woman back at home have shut up shop – all at once and just like that – and they're refusing to let their husbands in.

Magistrate   So how are you putting up with it?

Ambassador   It's very hard. All the men are trudging round the streets bent double with these massive protuberances like something that you'd hang your hat on. And as for the women – they won't let us within so much as touching distance of their sacred groves until we all unite in one resolution to bring peace to Greece.

Magistrate   What we've got's an international conspiracy among our women. That much is now clear. So, we must lose no time. We must convene a summit meeting here, with representatives from every state, each man with plenipotentiary decision-making powers. I'll go to parliament straight way and have them elect delegates. My wand of office will provide the requisite authority.

Ambassador   I'll do the same. Everything you said was hard straight talk.

Exeunt Magistrate *and* Ambassador. *Enter* Chorus of Old Women.

Old Men
A wildcat or a forest fire is easier to tame
Than an always blighting, always slighting, always fighting
dame.

Old Women

Well, if you know that and you've sense, you'd treat us with
kid-gloves.
Instead of making war with us, you could be making love.

Old Men

I've always hated women, and I'll hate them till I die.

Old Women

That's up to you. But look, you're cold and shivering, and I
Don't want to see you suffering. It's silly. So my vote is:
Hold out your arms for mummy and we'll dress you in your
coaties.

The Old Men *stretch out their arms. The* Old Women *start
caressing them.*

Old Men

I say, you know, that's rather nice. I'm feeling rather mellow.
I don't know what got into me. I've been a naughty fellow.

Old Women

Well now you must be a brave boy, and try hard not to cry
While I take out this little smut that's lodged here in your
eye.

Old Men

Yes please – it's been annoying me. Look, use this dampened
cloth.
And show it to me afterwards – it feels like a giant moth.

Old Women

Despite your being a naughty boy, I'll cure you well and proper
Right here we go. Gosh, look at that! *(removing the grit)* It
really is a whopper!

Old Men

You've cured me! It's been bugging me. It's such relief. That's
maybe

Why now it's out I just can't stop from crying like a baby.

Old Women
I'll dry your eyes, you silly scamp. I'll wash your tears away.
I'll kiss you.

Old Men   I don't want to kiss.

Old Women   I'll kiss you anyway!

The Old Women *give the* Old Men *a huge smacker of a kiss.*

Old Men
You get your own way every time, and, damn it, you're so
clever –
That's why we can't live with you but we'll live with you for
ever!
So let's make peace, shake hands and then we'll all be sitting
pretty
And altogether let's link arms and chant this little ditty:

The following can be sung by all, or spoken individually.

All
Now normally in comedies we'd look for some excuse
To pick on people in posh seats and shower them with abuse.
But everything's reversed today, so you can all relax –
We've all endured enough, you see, with this wretched war
tax.
But now we've occupied the bank, whoever's had a tax demand
Can help themselves to what they want – five, ten, a hundred
grand!
And when peace comes, don't worry if they summon you to
court –
With this inflation, what you owe will be exactly naught.

We're going to celebrate tonight. We'll have a slap-up dinner.
And we'll ask all our friends along, 'cos everyone's a winner.
We're having pâté de foie gras and langoustines and caviare,

And suckling pig with truffles, boeuf en daube and steak
tartare.
So, get into your glad rags, come on down, but don't you worry!
We won't be letting you in. So, fuck off, and buy a curry!

Look, here's our shaggy Spartan friends coming back.
Looks like they've been foraging and picked up a cock or
two on the way. Gentlemen, welcome. Have you any hard
news for us?

Enter the Spartan Ambassador *and his entourage.*

Ambassador No need for a long report. You can tell how
things stand just by looking at us.

Old Men I say! You *are* stretched, aren't you! I'd say the
situation was somewhat inflamed.

Ambassador You're telling me. I'm bursting to make peace
with anyone anytime anywhere!

Old Men Look, here's our own representative arriving. A fine
athletic fellow, though clearly suffering from muscle strain.

Enter Magistrate.

Magistrate I don't think that we can take this for much
longer. Look what a state I'm in! Where's Lucy?

Old Men What a state *you're* in? Look at this – it's a pandemic!
When do you feel the symptoms most – in the morning, when
you waken up?

Magistrate All the time – and the swelling's so raw. If we can't
find anything to bring it down, we'll all be queuing round the
back to go through the keyhole with Julian Clary*.

---

* Substitute as necessary a current famous gay celebrity and reference.

Old Men Best to keep your affliction hidden. Don't want any-one getting the wrong end of the stick.

Magistrate No, no – you're right. Don't want to flaunt it.

Ambassador Ah, yes – I seem to have popped out for a bit, too. There, that's better!

Magistrate Oh, hello – it's you, is it? The Spartan. We're all in a sticky situation.

Ambassador You're telling me. And out in public like this – I just feel so exposed. And they're such stiff negotiations.

Magistrate Right then. Let's get straight to the bottom of things – I mean let's get straight to the point. What's the purpose of this summit?

Ambassador To make peace.

Magistrate Absolutely – I second that. So let's bring Lucy in – the whole outcome of these talks is in her hands.

Ambassador Lucy it is.

Magistrate And, look – no need to fetch her. Here she is. Right on cue.

Enter Lucy.

Old Women
Screw to the sticking place your heart, o best and bravest Lucy,
It's time to be both sweet and tart, to be both tough and juicy,
Both flexible and rigid too, rub smooth the rough, fill in cracks,
The fate of Greece is in your hands, and fast approaching climax.

Lucy *(to* Old Women) The trick is to get in there while the situation's still inflamed but there's still no outcome. We'll

145

soon see if I'm right. *(to all)* Ladies and Gentlemen, I give you Molly – Molly Fication.

Enter Molly, *a stunning young woman. Many scholars like to think of her as being played by a real naked girl.*

Lucy *(to* Molly*)* First bring the Spartans here to me – but don't be rough with them. Just because that's how some Neanderthals like to treat their women, there's no need for us to do the same. No, take them gently, softly by the hand – the way we women like it. If they won't give you their hand, just grab them by the prick! Now, bring me the Athenians – just take hold of whatever presents itself. *(*Molly *does as requested.)* Spartans, you stand here. Athenians, stand there. And listen to what I'm going to say.

I know I have the body but of a weak and feeble woman; but I'm not a fool. I have my own intelligence. I have a knowledge and an understanding learned both from my father and from all the weight of all the generations which have gone before. And if my words find fault, they find fault not with one side or the other, but with you all, and rightly – with you all who share one country and one history, one family, all of you, all Greeks all worshipping as one, competing all as one in the Olympic Games, with all of your achievements, Delphi and Thermopylae, art, architecture, literature, this special, wonderful, so fragile glory that is Greece – our enemies are arming themselves even as we speak, and what do you do? Slaughter Greek men, sack Greek cities. In the catalogue of my complaints, take this as my first entry.

Magistrate If I don't make an entry soon, I'm going to die!

Lucy Now, moving on to each side individually. You Spartans will recall the time when you thought all was lost with you, when your continuing existence hung by the merest thread, threatened by unrest and revolution. And, when it seemed things were as bad as they could ever be, an earthquake devastated Sparta. Do you remember? Yes, of course you do. What did you do then? What did you do? You came to us for help, to Athens, and we mobilised the army and we sent our boys out and we saved you. We saved Sparta. And what have you done in return? You've burnt our land and villages. You've turned our land to ash. What gratitude!

Magistrate God yes, they're guilty, Luce!

Ambassador God, yes, we're guilty – but look at that! *(Pointing to* Molly*) Phoaa*! That's what I call a nice firm arse!

Lucy And turning now to the Athenians: have you forgotten what you owe the Spartans? Have you forgotten how, when Athens was in danger of being crushed by a dictatorship, the only people who stood by you were the Spartans? How the Spartans rallied round, and routed the dictators and their mercenaries? Have you forgotten that your freedom, your democracy, that everything you cherish and hold dear, you have today because of them, the Spartans? Have you forgotten that?

Ambassador What a forthright little woman!

Magistrate *(Pointing to* Molly*)* What a fine tight little cunt!

Lucy Why are you fighting when you owe each other everything? Why can you not make peace? Why can't you talk, negotiate? Please! What's so difficult?

Ambassador We're definitely ready – it's just a question of, well how might one put it delicately, I mean a question, or a matter that is, yes a matter of ifs and buts ...

Lucy Of ifs and buts?

Ambassador Well not so much the ifs, as the buts. *(Looking at* Molly*) This* butt, in fact. It's a matter of this butt – we've had our eye on it for some time, and what we really want to do is get our hands on it.

Magistrate No! Never! It's unnatural!

Lucy If that's the way they want it, let them have it.

Magistrate But, where do we come in?

Lucy There *are other ways*. But take your time. When it comes to negotiations, it's important to choose your point of entry carefully.

Magistrate All right, then. (*Using* Molly*'s body as a demonstration aid*.) We'll start here with these gently curving hills, and move on down along the plain here, circling this mound, like this, to slip into this anchorage ...

Ambassador No, no – not there!

Lucy Oh, let him! He's got to get his point in somehow!

Magistrate I'm ready to strip off and do some hoeing!

Ambassador For me, it's uphill gardening every time.

Lucy Well, once you've signed the treaty and made peace, you can do whatever you want. But if that *is* what you want to do, go and consult your allies and agree your terms.

Magistrate No need for that! We've reached to point of no return. And all we want's to come together in true diplomatic intercourse!

Ambassador God, yes – we're up for that!

Magistrate Man and boy, through thick and thin!

Lucy Well said! Now, go and purify yourselves – no, look, you need a shower! – and when you come back we women will entertain you with all the honey-sweet delights found only in our boxes. So, make your oaths and promises, sign on the dotted line, and then each one of you can take the woman of his choice … and away you go!

Magistrate I won't be a minute!

Ambassador Me neither!

Magistrate In fact, I'll be less than a minute!

Exeunt all except for Choruses.

Chorus
Prada, Paul Smith, Jasper Conran
Quant or Dior or Ralph Lauren –
It's party time, and if I'm able
I'll make damn sure that I wear a label.

'Cos we're back in the party world – don't get me wrong –
The door's been closed for too bloody long.
But the time is now and the time has come for pleasure
So open up my box and enjoy my treasure.

But there's one thing that I would advise:
Don't always trust what you see with your own eyes.
You may think that it's a pussy up there shaking her tail,
But remember this is Athens – it could easily be male.

Hey – you hungry? I've got food galore.
I've got pies and I've got pastries and a whole lot more.
So come over! Help yourself and please don't wait till I invite you!
But remember I've a pit bull and the fucker's sure to bite you.

Enter 1st Hoodie, *clutching a custard pie. One of the* Chorus of Old Men *takes the role of doorkeeper.*

1st Hoodie Open up! Open up!

Doorkeeper Bugger off!

1st Hoodie What are you doing sitting there anyway? I know how to get you going. Custard pies, that how!

Doorkeeper Oh, not the custard pie routine. It's such an old gag. I really don't want to do that one.

1st Hoodie No, you're right. Let's leave it. But – I think, the audience would like us to do it?

Enter 2nd Hoodie, *also clutching a custard pie.*

2nd Hoodie I'd like us to do it too!

They try to press their pies on the Doorkeeper's *face. He ducks. They pie each other.*

Doorkeeper Look, fuck off, won't you? Long-haired layabouts. The Spartans are coming and we don't want any trouble.

Exeunt Hoodies. *Enter two* Diners, *very inebriated.*

1st Diner Thass the bess party that I've ever been to. And those Spartans are really very entertaining. Very entertaining indeed. And we were pretty smart ourselves, you know. Specially after we'd had a little drinky or two.

2nd Diner Well we're certainly not smart when we're sober. If they took my advice, our negotiators would never go anywhere until they were well and truly plastered. I mean, look what happens normally – we go off to our summit meetings hideously sober, and spend all our time looking for tricks and complications. We don't listen to what they do say, and we get suspicious about anything they *don't* say, and so the public statements afterwards bear absolutely no relation to reality whatsoever. But when you've had a few, it all makes perfect sense. If we start singing '*Roll Me Over in the Clover*' when they've asked for '*She Was Only a Publican's Daughter*', we find it doesn't really matter, 'cos the publican's daughter's in clo-

ver anyway. You see? Oh, thank God for that – the rest of
them are coming back on stage. Cue our exit.

1st Diner Yes – here they come!

Exeunt Diners. *Enter* Ambassador, Magistrate, Lucy *and all
other main characters.*

Ambassador Now, you're a sweet little thing, and you're going
to accompany me, aren't you? On the flute. I can feel a dance
coming on, and a song in praise of Athens and Sparta.

Magistrate For God's sake, music! Yes! And dance!

Ambassador
  It's really quite a mystery
  When you think of all our history
  And everything that's gone before –
  Why ever did we start this war?

Magistrate
  Take Athens, plucky little state,
  Backs to the wall, defying fate
  She smashed the Persian ships at sea
  And still got home in time for tea.

Ambassador
  And Sparta played her part as well
  As any schoolroom swot will tell:
  She sent three hundred men to die
  To save Greece at Thermopylae.

Magistrate
  All these historic references
  Suggest we shelve our differences
  Because, you see, it's only fair
  We concentrate on what we share.

151

Ambassador
> So, on this most auspicious day
> Let's raise a toast, and let us pray
> That these words resonate through Greece:
> The war is over!

Both Let's make peace!

Lucy Well, all that's gone off very nicely. *(She indicates that the men and women should join together.)* Spartans, your wives. Athenians, *your* wives. So, now we're all together again, let's stand by our partners and join in ritual dance and pray that never again will we succumb to such madness.

They all dance as they sing the following song:

Chorus
> Peace to Greece and peace that blesses
> All its gods and its goddesses
> Zeus and Hera, and the mighty
> Bacchus, Ares, Aphrodite,
> Old Hephaestus with his knock-knees,
> Demeter, Poseidon, Hermes,
> Siblings Artemis, Apollo,
> Great Athene whom we follow,
> Peace to all! Be safe and happy!
> Now bring some booze and make it snappy!

They stop dancing, applaud and start to drink.

Lucy Now, what about a nice Spartan song?

Again, they all dance, singing as they do:

Chorus
> In all of Greece there's none that's smarter
> Than your citizen of Sparta,
> And these days it is quite a tonic
> To find a man who's so laconic.

Need a friend? One who will hearten?
Look no further than your Spartan.
He's always brave. He's never yellow.
Your Spartan's such a splendid fellow!
So, taking everything together
I want to be his friend for ever!

Just one last thing, before we go –
Something everyone should know:
With her golden hair
And her warlike stare
And her big bronze shield
That she likes to wield
And her owl
With the scowl
(Such a clever little fowl)
And the gorgon's head that rattles
In the clattering of battles
There's one goddess we all fear
And she's not so far from here.
She's Athene and we praise her
And the whole of Greece obeys her –
Athens, Sparta, all the cities –
And we pray now that she pities
Us and blesses our uniting
'Cos we've had enough of fighting.

The dance ends in the curtain call.

Suggested Further Reading

Greek comedy in general

M. Revermann (ed.), *The Cambridge Companion to Greek Comedy* (forthcoming 2011).

Aristophanic comedy

Bowie, A.M., *Aristophanes, Myth, Ritual and Comedy* (Cambridge: Cambridge University Press, 1996).

Cartledge, P., *Aristophanes and his Theatre of the Absurd* (Bristol: Bristol Classical Press, 1991).

Dover, K.J., *Aristophanic Comedy* (Berkeley: University of California Press, 1992).

Hubbard, T.K., *The Mask of Comedy: Aristophanes and the Intertextual Parabasis* (Ithaca NY: Cornell University Press, 1991).

MacDowell, D.M., *Aristophanes and Athens, an Introduction to the Plays* (Oxford: Oxford University Press, 1995).

Reckford, K.J., *Aristophanes' Old-and-New Comedy* (Durham NC: University of North Carolina Press, 1987).

Revermann, M., *Comic Business: Theatricality, Dramatic Technique, and Performance Contexts of Aristophanic Comedy* (Oxford: Oxford University Press, 2006).

Robson, J., *Aristophanes: An Introduction* (London: Duckworth, 2009).

Segal, E., *Oxford Readings in Aristophanes* (Oxford: Oxford University Press, 1996).

Silk, M.S., *Aristophanes and the Definitions of Comedy* (Oxford: Oxford University Press, 2002).

Editions of *Lysistrata*

Henderson, J., *Lysistrata* (Oxford: Clarendon Press, 1990).

Sommerstein, A., *Lysistrata* (Warminster: Aris and Phillips, 1990).

English translations and versions of *Lysistrata*

Fitts, D., *Aristophanes: Four Comedies* (New York: Mariner Books, 2003).

Halliwell, S., *Aristophanes Birds, Lysistrata, Assembly Women, Wealth* (Oxford: Clarendon Press, 1997).

Henderson, J., *Staging Women: 'Lysistrata', 'Women at the Thesmorphoria' and 'Assemblywomen': Three Plays by Aristophanes* (London: Routledge, 1996).

McLaughlin, E., *The Greek Plays* (New York: Theatre Communications Group Inc., 2006).

Sommerstein, A., *Lysistrata and Other Plays* (Harmondsworth: Penguin, 2003).

For information about individual productions of *Lysistrata*, go to the Archive of Performances of Greek and Roman Drama (http://www.apgrd.ox.ac.uk).

Index

This index is to the Introduction and Essays.
References to notes are in *italics*.

Index

Index

Index

Sparta, 2-5, 7-9, 12-13, 38-44, 48-9, 53-6, 60-1, 69
Spartans, 3-5, 7, 21, 26, 29, 32-4, 39-43, 45-9, 53-7, 59, 62, 66-9, 75-6, 84, 88
Symposium (Plato), 5, 7-8
Syracuse, 3

Thebes, 9, 29
Thermopylae, 6, 39
Theseus, 26
Thesmophoria, 17, 21
Thesmophoriazusae, 16, *27*
Thiercy, Pascal, 37
Thucydides, 21, 23, *28*, 31, *36*, 43, 45, 55, 61
Tissaphernes, 4, 7
Trojan Women, 37
Troy, 29, 55
Turkey, 3
Tyrtaeus, 75

Versnel, H.S., 24-5
Vietnam, 19, 37, 71
Volonakis, Minos, 16

war, 2-5, 7-8, 11-13, 17-19, 20, 22, 26, 29, 31-2, 35-41, 47-8, 53, 67, 69, 73, 75-7, 81-5, 88
War (God of), 12, 19
War (Peloponnesian), 2-8, 12-13, 17-18, 21-2, 35-6, 38, 41, 45, 47-9, 53-5, 57, 59, 61, 63, 73, 76, 81, 84, 88
war (World Wars), 15, 19, 77
War on Terror, 19
warrior, 22-3, 26, 30-1, 37, 47, 73
Wealth, 47, 78
Wheelwright, Charles, 15

Zeus, 6-7, 24-6, 30, 47